T0167567

Biopolitical
Imperialism

Biopolitical
Imperialism

M. G. E. Kelly

Winchester, UK
Washington, USA

First published by Zero Books, 2015
Zero Books is an imprint of John Hunt Publishing Ltd., Laurel House, Station Approach,
Alresford, Hants, SO24 9JH, UK
office1@jhpbooks.net
www.johnhuntpublishing.com
www.zero-books.net

For distributor details and how to order please visit the 'Ordering' section on our website.

Text copyright: M. G. E. Kelly 2014

ISBN: 978 1 78279 132 4
Library of Congress Control Number: 2014956319

All rights reserved. Except for brief quotations in critical articles or reviews, no part of this book may be reproduced in any manner without prior written permission from the publishers.

The rights of M. G. E. Kelly as author have been asserted in accordance with the Copyright, Designs and Patents Act 1988.

A CIP catalogue record for this book is available from the British Library.

Design: Stuart Davies

Printed and bound by CPI Group (UK) Ltd, Croydon, CR0 4YY, UK

We operate a distinctive and ethical publishing philosophy in all areas of our business, from our global network of authors to production and worldwide distribution.

CONTENTS

-1

Prologue

As I was finishing this book, visceral demonstrations of its main theses occurred. During July 2014, two major events dominated world news: the shooting down of a Malaysia Airlines plane over Eastern Ukraine, and the slaughter of Palestinians by Israel (though the latter is typically reported as a 'conflict' between Israel and Hamas). In the former event, 298 people died. On the basis of a relatively tenuous connection (the plausible assumption that the plane was shot down using weaponry supplied by Russia), Western leaders and media were quick to accuse Russian president Vladimir Putin of responsibility and condemn him. The news solemnly intoned that the 'international community' is united against Russia. By contrast, in Palestine, in the most recent round of bombing, many times as many people, more than 2,000, were killed by the Israeli military, using weapons largely supplied and/or paid for by the United States. Not only does no one point the finger at President Obama for these atrocities, but he is rather cast as a peacemaker. Indeed, the killing itself, despite its different scale, is cast in an entirely different light, as a rational and inevitable reaction to a threat. The idea that people in Ukraine who shoot down planes are also defending themselves is not entertained, their spokespeople not interviewed.

What one sees here, mixed in with propaganda, is a differential valuation of life: some lives are deemed more important than others. The lives of the mostly Western passengers on the intercontinental jet are considered more important than those of the people whose homes they pass over, be they Russians or Arabs. The lives of Israeli citizens are considered so much more important than those of non-Israeli Palestinians that thousands of the latter can be killed simply to prevent deaths of a handful of the former. Even the cadavers of Australian citizens on the downed plane were deemed so important that armed Australian agents were dispatched to the scene, in the middle of a warzone, to aid in the recovery of these bodies, and the recovery operation was held in the media to be more important than the war it occurred in the midst of, a war in which thousands of people have died.

Now, it is unsurprising that the news media of a given country pays disproportionate attention to the lives of its own citizens. But the media—both in the First and the Third Worlds—also systematically elevate the significance of things that happen to foreign First World citizens. The greatest example of this effect were the '9/11' attacks on America in 2001, in which thousands of Americans perished, which was perhaps the biggest news story in history, an event with massive and far reaching consequences, far eclipsing the coverage and political consequences of much larger numbers of deaths elsewhere in the world. Of course, it was quite defensible for the world media to accord this event so much importance, since it had wide ranging repercussions for the world, precisely because of the US' titanic geopolitical weight. That is to say, the differential valuation of life is not merely a question of appearances but a structural reality. This book is about this differential valuation of life, how it is produced and enforced, and about some of its causes and consequences, not merely at the level of media representations, but as a practical matter of life and death.

What happened in Gaza is at once extreme and typical. It is a peculiarly stark case of a ubiquitous global phenomenon I call 'biopolitical imperialism'. Nowhere else in the world is a population kept alive by international aid donations to the extent that the people of Gaza are, although most of the poor populations of the world receive some such consideration. Nowhere else in the world today do the First and the Third Worlds sit so close together, though everywhere they are in direct contact. Nowhere else are the poor so directly oppressed by the rich, though inequality is everywhere inseparable from oppression: nowhere else do the wealthy slaughter the poor so directly, but, as I will argue, all rich countries are at least complicit in killing poor people outside their borders. Moreover, as in Israel, their explicit excuse for this killing is always to protect themselves, their own citizens, through a systemic overvaluation of the lives of their own people; Hamas's rockets, posing a negligible risk to Israeli civilians, more an inconvenience than an imminent threat to life, are deemed to justify the wholesale destruction of Palestinian neighbourhoods and infrastructure, burying whole families in rubble. Lastly, nowhere else in the world is the resistance of the oppressed so vigorous or sustained as in Palestine.

In light of the bloody disintegration of neighbouring Syria, where many times as many people have died than have died in Gaza, some argue that the focus of Western leftists on criticising Israel's killing of Palestinians overvalues Palestinian lives in a selective way. I would suggest the reason for their focus is not an overvaluation of Palestinian lives, however, but precisely that Israel is special in being the clearest example of contemporary biopolitical imperialism, where a Western First World population oppresses a Third World one directly and savagely. It is the proverbial visible tip of the iceberg. Israel is the only case today of an active project of settler colonialism still fighting to subjugate the native populace of its land, in contrast to settler colonies in the Americas and Australasia which have long since subjugated and/or assimilated first nations peoples. Israel is an extraordinarily raw spot on the body of global imperialism.

This means that Westerners singling out Israel is unfair, but only insofar as we criticise it without showing an awareness of the extent to which our countries are both essentially similar to Israel and complicit in its deeds. Several Western nations have bombed and killed Arab civilians in the last decade, all major

Western nations have a history of imperialism, and, I will argue, all Western nations are complicit in the broader strategy of imperialism. This includes, contemporarily, varying degrees of active support for Israel. This is particularly true of the dominant contemporary imperialist power, the United States of America, albeit with many willing helpers. We should criticise Zionism, but as a manifestation of a broader imperialism, rather than, as some have, most blatantly on the political far right, the engine of imperialism.

Since we are implicated in Israel's actions, it makes sense for us to protest against Israel, to demand that our governments act, since they have an involvement and influence in this situation. Specifically, we may demand our governments stop funding and supporting Israel. To the extent that our governments are supporting and funding killing in Syria—specifically by supporting the opposition—a similar demand might be made, though that support has been much less direct. In Gaza, since Israel does almost all of the killing, we can condemn and put pressure on Israel to stop. In Syria there is a civil war, in which we may enjoin the two sides to find a settlement, but the only thing that can be done from without is to intervene, that is, to make more war in the hope that this will somehow lead to less killing. Those who challenge leftists over Israel by making reference to Syria are in effect implying that we should be clamouring for our governments to intervene to help depose the Syrian government. The US and other governments were unabashedly keen to do this, their warmongering derailed by domestic and international opposition. Yet, the scale of death in Syria is already as attributable to outside intervention, in the form of funds and materiel and soldiers, as it is to a failure to intervene. Calls for intervention cannot be rationally motivated—though interveners sometimes claim it is—by a desire to save lives, but rather betray a callous disregard for them.

Support by our governments for both Israel and the Syrian

opposition is part of a strategy that proceeds from explicitly stated policy aims by the governments of the First World to secure, protect, and further their own interests and those of their people. This implies, though this is certainly not explicitly stated, that the lives of our citizens and friends are more important than those of our enemies or those of people who simply are in no particular way connected to us. What this entails in practice, I will argue—not logically, yet nonetheless consistently—is active harm to the lives, that is, ill health and deaths, of people elsewhere in the world. War is only the most visceral case of this effect; it is unfortunately only a relatively minor dimension of biopolitical imperialism, which encompasses the biological degradation of a large part of humanity through poverty and exploitation, through man-made disasters and preventable tragedies.

0

Toolkit

In this book, I will argue that, for the last hundred years at least, the people of the wealthiest countries in the world have been united behind their states via systems of care and cultivation—'biopolitics'—while these same states have actively inhibited the formation of similar biopolitics in the poorest parts of the world. This pattern is what I call 'biopolitical imperialism'. It amounts to the active (though not necessarily deliberate) destruction of the well-being of people in poor countries for the sake of the lives of people in wealthy countries. This formation is particularly distinctive of the late twentieth century, but continues today.

Before proceeding to show how this operates, I will introduce, in this chapter, the key terms in which my argument will be made, in particular the two parts of the eponymous 'biopolitical imperialism'. 'Biopolitics' needs to be explained because many will not be familiar with the concept at all—and even those who are may understand it differently to the way I will use it. 'Imperialism' is a word with more common currency, but it has multiple senses, and I use it here in quite a specific way.

0.1 Biopolitics

The word 'biopolitics' dates back to the early twentieth century.[1] The usage of the term in the contemporary academic humanities and social sciences, the context in which I write, however relates specifically to Michel Foucault's idiosyncratic usage of it in seminal work from 1976, namely the first volume of his *History of Sexuality* and his lecture series *Society Must Be Defended*. Foucault's usage has given rise in turn to tangentially related usages of the concept by three Italian philosophers in particular: Giorgio Agamben, Roberto Esposito, and Antonio Negri.

I will use the word specifically in the sense given to it by Foucault in 1976, not in the senses developed by later theorists. If there is an essential difference between Foucault's definition of the concept and those of its Italian adopters, it can be found in the etymological elaboration of the term, specifically in the determination of meaning of the prefix 'bio-'. Contemporary interpreters tend to trace this directly to its Greek root, *bios*, which is translatable as life, specifically human life. They thus define biopolitics as the politics of human life. However, it is then not obvious what distinguishes it from politics simpliciter, since there is no politics which does not relate directly to human life. This leads on the one hand to Agamben's identification of biopolitics with the entire history of Western politics, and on the other to the arbitrary use of the concept by Negri to mean any contemporary politics of resistance. These definitions render the concept useless, reducing it to a trendy buzzword.

Foucault by contrast gave the word a more—though not entirely—precise definition. In his usage, the 'bio-' of biopolitics is a contraction of 'biological'. For him, biopolitics arose when scientific reflection on life met politics. Biopolitics means government that takes into account the lives of people as a systematic calculation, utilising scientific knowledge.

Before the biopolitical era, in the medieval and early modern period, rulers did not do this. Monarchs only exceptionally levied taxes or conducted surveys, occasionally called people to fight for them, and occasionally slaughtered them when they displeased them. There was no science to such rule, only brutal technique.

Today, by contrast, governments in the 'advanced' countries monitor more or less everybody, in order ostensibly to ensure their well-being. This monitoring began in efforts to alleviate disease, to avert the national economic and military decline disease could precipitate. Dealing with disease effectively requires an approach that takes in the whole population. Later, proto-economists posited a direct correlation of the number of people in a country to its wealth, motivating governmental interventions to regulate the size of the population through measures other than disease control. This led to a constitution of the population as an object of government attention, and a genuine concern with its well-being becoming central to governing practice.

Biopolitics is a form of power that controls by using scientific knowledge to care for and enhance the lives of entire populations. In biopolitical societies, our health is looked after, not as a matter of pure charitable concern (though this is part of the story), but in order to enhance the power of the state and the wealthy. That is not to cast biopolitics in an exclusively negative light, however: it would seem to benefit everyone. Moreover it is not simply imposed from above, but is something actively fought for and brought about by the efforts of ordinary people. It should indeed be understood as coming into being through complex mutual incitement, involving antagonistic struggle between different social forces.

This process does have its dark side. Foucault claims that, by producing a coherent population, biopolitics ushers in an era of unprecedentedly bloody warfare, in which entire populations are pitted against each other in an apparent struggle for survival. Rather than clashes between armies, we see 'total war', with millions of men under arms and the destruction of entire cities behind the lines. This, for Foucault, is made possible in biopolitics on the basis of an incipient 'state racism' which mediates between the politics of death and that of life, justifying the death of others for the sake of the health of the population. It is in this way, I will argue, that biopolitical imperialism operates.

0.2 Imperialism

In its ordinary sense, 'imperialism' means the creation of empires, as seen in the late nineteenth century, when every great power sought to acquire colonies. 'Colonialism' is the word I will use to refer to this phenomenon, reserving 'imperialism' for something more specific, namely a sense of the word developed by Marxists, most influentially—though by no means originally—by Lenin, who, as leader of the Russian Revolution, became the defining thinker of twentieth century Marxism.[2]

The word 'colonial' comes from the Latin *colonia*, colonial settlements in the Roman Empire composed of former soldiers, established as a means of controlling conquered areas, while also providing an incentive to soldiers to fight to conquer these areas. This colonialism, settlement of conquered territories, appropriation of land for farming, enslavement of local inhabitants, was also the main pattern of European imperial expansion from the sixteenth to eighteenth centuries, but European expansion during the nineteenth century was so extensive it also created 'colonies' where no serious attempt to colonise was made, namely in South and South-East Asia, and West Africa. Certainly significant numbers of Europeans did settle in these regions, but settlement was not the point of this colonisation, and the Europeans were always greatly outnumbered by indigenous inhabitants. The point was rather primarily commercial and sometimes military: it was to open markets to trade, plunder natural resources, and to prevent other Europeans from doing the same.

The word 'imperialism', on the other hand, was used by Lenin to refer to a distinctive economic phenomenon that occurred during this colonial period: a change in capitalism from the dominance of industrial capital (that is, making money by producing and selling things) to the dominance of finance capital (making money from money by investing it). For Lenin the decisive shift occurred at the beginning of the twentieth century. Empire had initially been about capturing goods and land, had then become a means for securing captive markets to sell one's goods, but now became financialised, a matter of securing investment opportunities. As it turned out, this shift would make colonialism redundant.

The decline of European colonial empires had multiple causes. Certainly, it could not have happened without the resistance of the colonised, which grew to a point where it made colonialism unprofitable in many regions. A factor in the opposite direction was the exhaustion of European powers in two massive conflagrations, which meant they had fewer reserves to impose their will on other lands. This catalysed the emergence and growth of a Communist bloc which supported anti-imperialist struggles materially and ideologically. In this context, the idea that colonialism was unjust became hegemonic. This idea took hold not only because of the rise of Communism, but partly because of the newly dominant influence of America after the Second World War. As a state which itself threw off British colonial rule, America has presented itself as having a different attitude to colonialism; although it itself seized colonies from Spain at the end of the nineteenth century, it allowed its largest overseas colony, the Philippines, to become independent during the twentieth. America's opposition to colonialism was as much pragmatic as principled, however: it could not allow its minor partners to maintain vast global empires. After all, the purpose of European colonial empires had always largely been to achieve monopolies for the power's companies, and America now wanted favoured access to all markets for itself. Effectively, the Monroe Doctrine, by which the US had opposed any European colonialism in Central and South America, was now applied to the entire world.

This confluence of factors meant that, between the end of World War Two and the 1960s, European powers were forced to withdraw wholesale from their colonial possessions. Only Portugal retained substantial territorial colonies after this time, fighting costly protracted wars leading in 1974 to a metropolitan revolution and a new regime that abandoned empire. There had been an earlier mass loss of European colonial possessions, namely in the Americas: between the American Declaration of Independence in 1776 and Independence of Brazil in 1822, the great majority of the New World passed from European suzerainty to independence. The difference between the two bouts of decolonisation is that in the earlier case—except in Haiti—local power was won by ethnic European settlers, whereas in twentieth century decolonisation, political power passed, at least officially, to native elites, not least because most of the colonies concerned had not been settler colonies.

Decolonisation has not led to an end of imperialism in Lenin's sense, however. Rather, finance capital has clearly become ever more dominant. Twentieth century decolonisation was military and political, but did not necessarily involve divestment of economic influence. While many former colonies did attempt to curtail the commercial operations of imperialist powers, over the last half century the barriers to exploitative imperialist economic relations have been worn down again almost everywhere. Thus, formal decolonisation conceals continuing economic dependency and subjugation. The post-colonial order by now amounts to a victory for imperialism: the expense of maintaining the boots on the ground has been largely dispensed with, while the economic benefits continue to flow to the old imperial powers.

Lenin characterises imperialism as a form of parasitism, in which the imperialist nation lives off its colonies. In this much it resembles a common image of the capitalist ruling class living parasitically off the labour of the workers within its own country. The surprising thing in Lenin's picture of imperialism, repressed by most contemporary readers, is that he characterises not just the ruling class of the imperialist nation as parasitic, but the imperialist nation itself, potentially including its working class. While the workers inside a country are exploited by their employers, the workers of the colonies are super-exploited, suffering additional exploitation, which accrues potentially not only to the imperialist elite, but to most of the population of the imperialist metropole. Lenin is particularly influenced here by the English liberal economist John A. Hobson, who envisions an elite of massively wealthy rentiers living off the profit generated by imperialism and employing much of the rest of the population of their country to service their needs, the latter living the life of pampered servants, accomplices cut in on the imperialist deal, with a federation of Western states combining together to exploit the rest of the world. Lenin argued that this would happen were it not for the considerable resistance imperialism occasioned. However, with the increasing circumvention of this resistance in the course of the twentieth century precisely via the tactic of decolonisation, I would argue that this scenario has been at least partially realised in Western countries in which the finance sector has become the heart of the economy, and the service sector the one in which most people actually work. The UK is a case in point here: in less than a century it went from being the industrial powerhouse of the world, to a country which produces relatively little.

One means by which ordinary people in the First World benefit from imperialism, not explicitly recognised by Lenin, is illuminated by Arghiri Emmanuel's unequal exchange thesis. This, stated simply, says that super-exploitation occurs due to wage differentials. An average Indian worker earns perhaps 1% of what a Western worker does for the same amount of work. The Western worker may thus purchase a hundred days of the Indian's labour for only one day of his own labour. Such a trade is rarely made explicit, but every time a Western worker buys something made in India, she gets an effective 99% discount on the manufacturing labour component of the price. Conversely, if an Indian buys something made in the West, she must pay a hundred times more for the Western labour embodied in it than her own labour is worth.

There are many reasons why the First World is wealthier than

poor countries: firstly, and most anciently, primitive acquisition—effectively simple theft—of resources, which still occurs
today to some extent; unequal exchange, secured on the basis of
technological advantage, some goods being available only from
advanced countries, hence being able to command grossly
inflated prices; military might, used to enforce disadvantageous
trading conditions—the possibility of such force being itself
largely premised on a technological disparity; the financialisation of the global economy, by which rents have displaced
trade as a major driver of advanced economies; and lastly, as an
effect of this, the running of continuous current account deficits
based on the perceived desirability of supporting First World
debts, allowing the importation of even more goods than it is
possible to acquire through primitive acquisition and unequal
exchange. Each of these engines can be said to be unsustainable
to some degree. Technological and (hence) military advantage
can be eroded in various ways, and at some point mountains of
debt may come crashing down. These phenomena may stand or
fall together: debt obligations can only be enforced while the
imperialist countries maintain a towering power advantage.

0.3 Global Divisions

Some argue today that the notion of 'imperialism' is out-dated,
since imperialism has been superseded by 'globalisation', the
erosion of national boundaries in relation to commerce and
migration, meaning that there is no clear division between centre
and periphery. At the turn of the millennium, this argument was
perhaps more prominent than today, its key text provided by
Michael Hardt and Antonio Negri's *Empire*. With America's 2003
invasion of Iraq in the face of protests from much of the world,
however, even Hardt and Negri were forced to reconsider their
thesis,[3] rumours of imperialism's demise seeming suddenly
exaggerated.

Certainly, in the century since Lenin wrote, the extent to

which there are distinct national capitals has declined: the capitalists of a given country no longer unite to the same extent to compete against capitalists from elsewhere. In Europe in particular there has been a sea change from murderous competition between nations to commercial integration. This is in no small part due to the spread of ownership of companies across national borders. The extent of this transnationalisation of capital is often exaggerated, however: so called transnational corporations (TNCs) may operate across many borders, but they are usually attached to one or at most a couple of countries in the primary location of their ownership and management (even if their taxes are filed elsewhere). We may refer to two different transnationalisations: a genuine globalisation of the operations of many corporations, while the headquarters and shareholders have been transnationalised to a lesser extent, remaining largely within the First World, though there are increasingly exceptions to this pattern. Via the second transnationalisation, the First World increasingly operates like a cohesive whole (though national differences stubbornly remain within this on certain questions), a tendency Karl Kautsky dubbed 'ultraimperialism'. This clubbing together to dominate the world dates back to the victory in the Second World War of an alliance of capitalist powers, that went on to constitute itself after the war as the OECD and Nato, joining forces with its defeated adversaries Japan and Germany to compose a bloc against international Communism. The end of the Cold War saw this agglomeration globally triumphant and expansive. Today, the richest states have cosy reciprocal relations with one another, maintaining a relationship of collective parasitism with the rest of the world. Multiple tendencies threaten this pattern, however, as is always the case in any complex social formation.

There is indeed a general geopolitical trend towards globalisation, rendering nations less important than they once were, but not to the point that imperialism is decisively ended. The division between sectors of the globe has never been absolute. As in the divisions between classes in a society, where concrete individuals' situations show considerable variation in a continuum, the overall pattern of division is stark. The difference between a rich person and a poor person is not negated by the fact that there is a continuum of people in between. This holds true within a society—the difference between a financier and an impoverished welfare recipient is immediately perceptible, even in the most 'social democratic' country—and globally: the difference between a poor person from a Western nation and an Indian slum-dweller is also unmistakable. The benefit payments of the poorest in Britain amount to approximately a hundred times the income of ordinary Indians, which is the difference between the incomes of people in the lowest and highest deciles within the UK. Benefit claimants in Britain have clothes, phones, housing, and amenities beyond the reach of the majority of Indians. Those below the poverty line in advanced societies are by almost any measure within the top 10% of the world population. These are economic measures, but biological indicators follow a similar pattern, if less stark globally: the rich in London live a quarter of a century longer on average than the poor;[4] by contrast, the average Briton lives 15 years longer than the average Indian.

There are various ways of conceptualising this global division. We can speak of rich countries and poor countries. But this way of talking seems to imply that the division between the two is incidental and relative, and merely economic: some people and countries just happen to be rich, others poor. Since it is a systemic relationship, a more precise terminology is called for. Within a society, this is accomplished with the notion of class. Internationally, the terminology is more vexed. The dominant formal vocabulary today divides the world between 'developed' and 'developing' or 'underdeveloped' countries. This is pernicious, because it presupposes that all countries automatically 'develop' in the same way, and that all countries are actually on this pathway to 'development'. The same problem besets the division of the world into 'industrialised' countries and others, with the additional problem that the richest countries today seem to be less industrial than some poorer ones.

Other categorisations divide the world spatially: the 'West' is a prevalent descriptor, but much of the Western hemisphere is relatively poor, and parts of the East are quite wealthy. The term 'Global South' for the poorer countries captures the relation of wealthy North America vis-à-vis poor Latin America and wealthy Europe vis-à-vis poor Africa, but it works less well in the Eastern hemisphere: I am writing in Australia, one of the wealthiest countries in the world, named for its quintessential southernness. Still, I will use both these geographical designations on occasion.

Theorists of imperialism typically adopt neither the simple geographical nor the developmentalist vocabulary, in favour of alternative spatialisations. One such is to speak of a wealthy 'core' or 'metropole' and a poor 'periphery'. Another terminology, standard among scholars in the 1970s, but these days abandoned by them for the most part, is that of the First, Second and Third Worlds. These terms were originally used on the basis that in addition to the two poles of the Cold War, the First World being the capitalist West and the Second being the Communist East, there was a host of poor countries that constituted a third bloc. This idea seems obsolete given the arguable disappearance of the Second World, which sat between the richest and poorest regions economically. I nevertheless will primarily use this vocabulary. This is partly because these terms 'First World' and 'Third World' have today become the main colloquial way of referring to rich and poor countries respectively.

I also think they capture the extremity of the gap between the richest and poorest countries. My method here will be to make generalisations about the relationship between the richest and poorest countries in the world. When I say, 'First World', I mean principally the G7, and also smaller Western countries with very high per capita GDP, such as Australia and Switzerland, whereas I construe 'Third World' to include minimally most African countries and South Asia. I see the relationship of First World to Third World countries on this definition as offering a paradigm of how imperialism works. I acknowledge, however, that much of the world today offers rather more complicated, mixed situations. I will also discuss these, particularly the crucial case of China.

A further reason to invoke the concept of the Third World is that it has historically operated at times as a positive rallying point for anti-imperialism, as a collective identity for solidary action by poor and oppressed nations. While the concept may seem redundant from precisely this point of view, it is worth noting that the concept originated not in the Third World, but in the First as a description of the Third, and only then became a rallying cry. We may thus retain the umbrella term 'Third World' as a possible counterpoint precisely insofar as the exclusion of the Third World as such can give rise to a form of solidarity by which the Third World might develop what we might in quasi-Marxist terms call a 'world consciousness' of itself.

0.4 Biopolitical Imperialism

It is impossible in this book to consider the economic dimension of imperialism adequately, hence the thesis of economic imperialism forms a background which will be referred to, but which is not essential to my core conclusions. My remit is quite different, namely the specifically biopolitical dimension of imperialism. That said, biopolitics and economics are far from separate. As I have indicated, biopolitics emerged partially to serve economic motives, and it continues both to serve economic needs and to be supported by the economy. I will nevertheless claim that there is a specifically biopolitical parasitism at work. Indeed, we may posit a profusion of different dimensions of imperialism which all interlock and complement one another, not only economic and biopolitical, but also political, cultural, military, and epistemic. Imperialism can be defined economically in terms of capital flows from outside in or, for example, militarily by the ability to project military power across the world—the premier contemporary example of this is the US, which until this decade accounted for more than 50% of all of the world's military spending, and which divides the entire world into various spheres of operation, within any of which it can act on short notice. It can also be defined culturally, in terms of the flow outwards of cultural artefacts and tropes, for example the influence of Hollywood movies and Western pop songs. And it can be defined biopolitically.

One might imagine that biopolitical imperialism would mean a flow of biopolitics itself outward into the periphery. I will argue that, though some movement in this direction does exist, it is not the main way in which biopolitical imperialism operates. Imperialism is a form of power that by and large does not care about the lives of its victims. Imperialism, therefore, is primarily thanatopolitical, a politics of death, contrasting with the biopolitics of the population found within the imperial metropole. There is, I will contend, a direct relation between the two things, in which death is figuratively exported and life imported back, in a systematic degradation of the possibilities for biopolitics in the periphery, arising out of the operation of biopolitics in the centre. Thus, this book will proceed first by examining the constitution of the central population through biopolitical nationalism before mapping its relations fanning outward.

According to Foucault, thanatopolitics and biopolitics are applied differentially according to a logic that can be broadly described as 'racist', which separates those who are protected from those who can be killed. Biopolitical imperialism follows precisely such a racist logic, dividing the core populations of First

18

World citizens whose lives are deemed important from an expendable mass of humanity outside. This relates in complex ways, as we will see, to what we ordinarily call 'racism'.

I will argue that biopolitics constitutes a missing link in explaining how imperialism involves the ordinary people of the First World. For one thing, biopolitics provides a mechanism by which the profits of imperialism may be spread to a whole population. By uniting us in a single population, moreover, biopolitics generates solidarity between ordinary people and elites.

At the other pole, in the Third World, I will argue that there are specifically biopolitical forms of parasitism, involving the importation of life, for example via the current international migration regime, by which rich and well-qualified people from poor countries, particularly medical personnel, are drawn into wealthier populations. There is also a converse export industry of death, in which arms are sold to and used against people in poor countries, not only killing them, but also destroying the bases for the constitution of social insurance systems, preventing development. While rich nations claim to be helping poor nations to develop via 'aid', I will argue that this too tends to retard the development of national self-sufficiency in poor countries, while being in any case so small in scale as to be dwarfed within the relationship between First World and Third by the flow in the opposite direction.

0.5 Methodology

This book combines two concepts, which come from different places: Marxism and Foucault. I do not propose a hybrid methodology, however, so much as an essentially Foucauldian one. In particular, I understand imperialism itself in a specifically Foucauldian way, as a 'strategy of power', to use Foucault's parlance. This implies that it is a regular pattern with a certain directedness of its own, but without anyone involved in it themselves necessarily either understanding or intending its effects. I also follow his methodology in other ways. For one thing, I refuse to offer solutions to the problems I outline, since these cannot be prefigured in advance due to the epistemic opacity of the future, although I will examine some potential avenues of action for resisting the things I describe. I similarly eschew normative evaluations: like Foucault I seek primarily simply to analyse and show connections that have gone unnoticed. Another thing I take from Foucault is the premise that there is no particular aetiological primacy between different dimensions of a problem e.g. between culture, politics, and economics. All are important, all are interdependent, and all are distinct. Like Foucault's works, this one is intended as a specific contribution, describing an aspect of a problem: I am not attempting to reduce imperialism to biopolitics, to claim that imperialism or biopolitics are the central political problems today, only to identify an aspect of things that I think is not widely appreciated as such, though of course one may infer from my focus on certain questions that these do seem to be of particular importance to me.

I also follow Foucault in rejecting organicism, not viewing imperialism or the state as something like an organism. As Esposito points out, the word 'biopolitics' was itself originally coined by organicist theorists to mean politics as itself biological[5]—but I do not use the word in that way. Though I sometimes use the word 'system', I do not mean it in the organicist sense in which it is used in systems theory. Nevertheless, I do use the organic notion of 'parasitism', which does seem to me accurately to describe the situation insofar as the poor countries do not require the rich ones and simply suffer through their relations to them, though states and populations cannot literally be parasites inasmuch as they are not organisms.

I do diverge from Foucault's practice in some ways, of course. Trivially, I take a different historical frame to Foucault: where he tended to stop with the nineteenth century, that is where this study begins, and I am concerned to include current trends. I also try to deal with 'facts', where he dealt with archival discourses themselves (though hardly avoiding reference to concrete reality).

In what follows, I will map biopolitical imperialism centripetally from the biopolitical constitution of the nation (Chapter 1), through its borders (Chapter 2), to the three major forms of biopolitical imperialism: the importation of life (which primarily refers to immigration into the rich countries, but includes also phenomena such as the trade in human body parts), dealt with under the heading of 'Traffic' (Chapter 3); the export of life, 'Aid' (Chapter 4); and the export of death, 'War' (Chapter 5). The concluding chapter will assess contemporary trends and prospects for resistance and transformation.

1

Nation

It is not the modern state which is 'egalitarian' but the modern (nationalist) nation-state, this equality having as its internal and external limits the national community and, as its essential content, the acts which signify it directly (particularly universal suffrage and political 'citizenship'). It is, first and foremost, an equality in respect of nationality. – Étienne Balibar

1.1 Docile Populations

The population was invented as the object of demographics, as something to be monitored and encouraged. This control constituted the population as a real thing, creating the basis for it to emerge as a subject, a community of mutual interest. From this point, biopolitics involved a symbiosis of population and state, supporting one another.

The biopolitical state cares for the whole population, rather than for particular individuals or groups: it does not provide benefits only to the ruling class, nor does it simply provide a safety net for the poor. It does these things, but they are not distinctive of biopolitics; rather, they are older, the former being a function of every class society, the latter long existing as charity, administered in medieval Europe by the Church. Medieval Christianity attempted to ameliorate poverty, but saw it as a congenital feature of human life. Biopolitics by contrast aims to cure social disorders as if they were diseases.

Biopolitics expanded and intensified during the nineteenth and twentieth centuries. This is seen most strikingly in the provision of healthcare, but also in social welfare services and the provision of housing. In Britain, to take one example, it reached its apogee in massive social programmes created after the Second World War. The largest and most emblematic of these is the National Health Service, founded in 1948 to provide free healthcare for all. With this measure, the British state became the cradle to grave carer for the great majority of citizens: we were, and still are, mostly born in NHS hospitals and mostly die in them too. Simultaneously with the NHS, a statutory payment was established by the 1948 National Assistance Act for anyone with a low enough income, supporting the healthy too, and indeed helping them to remain healthy by providing them with the means to feed, clothe and house themselves. The same imperative also guided the direct provision of housing. The clearance of unhealthy slums was nationally mandated from the 1930s, in favour of government-owned housing. Though much criticised since for destroying communities by relocating people, the explicit intention was tied to health, particularly the provision of modern bathrooms within the domicile. At its peak, approximately 40% of people in the UK lived in social housing.

Similar measures were established at different points in all Western countries, albeit with important differences. Healthcare in particular has been provided in quite different ways: while in Britain healthcare is paid for almost entirely out of general taxation, other countries adopted models based on insurance. In Germany, for example, healthcare is a matter of individual health insurance, albeit government-subsidised. This insurance is mandatory, so near-universal—only 0.2% of people legally resident in Germany lack it. A unique case is presented by the US, where the state took an interest in healthcare relatively late in the piece, and most healthcare has remained rigorously private. Only in the 1960s did Medicare and Medicaid together provide cover for large numbers of people not in work, and until 2013 a substantial layer of people (more than 15% of the legally resident population) were covered neither by government programmes nor by private insurance. This more than any other thing differentiated American biopolitics from that in other Western countries, by giving the state a more minor role in relation to the health of the population. America nonetheless had a mass biopolitics, with the state in a guiding, regulatory position. Moreover, recent changes (namely the Affordable Care Act, or 'Obamacare') have mandated universal health coverage and thereby increased the role of the state. In other countries, there has been an opposite trend. In Britain, more and more people have private health insurance and private concerns increasingly pervade the public system. We may note also the precipitous managed decline of public housing in the UK deliberately instigated by the Thatcher government, and the extent to which in a number of countries welfare payments have morphed into increasingly conditional 'workfare'. The general trend in the West with the ascendency of neoliberalism since circa 1980 has been for demands from the political right to push against biopolitics, characterising the welfare state as 'nannying', intruding on personal freedom. This has led to a more mitigated biopolitics. Still, in all Western countries, the government continues to play a key role in ensuring that people are housed, fed, treated for medical conditions, and kept alive and relatively healthy, in order to ensure the well-being of the whole social body. A person dying on the street is not merely an individual tragedy, but a vector of disease and disorder. It is safer to subsidise the indigent than to leave them to haunt our streets. This is not only an economic calculation (although it is one, and neoliberalism pushes economic reductivism in policymaking), but a question of what the population will tolerate: the population expects the state to care for the population of the country as such, even if there is a palpable recent tendency for people to cease to care about the poorest layer of society. That said, there is no telling how far neoliberalism might take us.

Biopolitics has never in the West been allowed to override capitalism's constitutive inequalities. But biopolitics is not simply produced by capitalism, in order to ensure its labour force is healthy. Certainly, it does have such advantageous effects for capital, and would scarcely have become so entrenched in capitalist society otherwise, but it has arisen through a complex compromise between capital and labour, by which the immiserating effects of capitalism are mitigated and class conflict is dampened.

1.2 Biopolitical Nationalism

How is biopolitical national insurance imperialist? Well, in and of itself, it is not, but it has historically emerged in the imperialist context.

The imperialist dimension of the biopolitical care of the population might be explained by casting it as a luxury only made possible by economic flows from poorer parts of the world. Avoiding detailed economic dimension, it suffices for our purposes to say that our biopolitics is premised on our economic wealth, that imperialism has at the very least enriched Western nations, and that the biopolitical welfare state provides a mechanism by which the super-profits of imperialism may be distributed throughout the metropolitan social body, rather than accruing only to those at the top. While it is today well recognised that money does not automatically 'trickle down' within a society from the richest to the poorest, biopolitics is a pump by which wealth can be redistributed, and indeed this has been an explicit goal of the social welfare state, even if contemporary political rhetoric and taxation regimes no longer retain such an aim.

An early form of such a mechanism, albeit perhaps too crude to classify as properly 'biopolitical', is the corn dole by which the Roman Empire gave basic subsistence to the denizens of its populous capital, ensuring popular support for the Emperor of the day. Biopolitics likewise uses a portion of the profits of empire (in contemporary imperialism, this would mean profits from foreign investments, unequal exchange, etc.) to keep the core population healthy and content. Of course today's structures and flows are much more circuitous than those of antiquity, which makes it possible to doubt whether imperialism exists at all, let alone that it funds welfare programmes. One could argue that ordinary people's standard of living in Western countries is attainable by a distribution of the existing national product without transfers from outside, but this raises further questions about the extent to which that product is really endogenous. I must leave open here, though, the economic questions of whether First World citizens receive an overall subsidy from imperialism and of whether their existence could be materially guaranteed by the local economy of the metropole without imperialist international relations.

What is pertinent from our point of view is not so much the question of how biopolitics is funded as its effects on the relation of population and state to one another. My claim is that it binds population and state together in opposition to their collective outside. The question of whether this is really in the overall economic interest of the population is prodigiously complex, but I will argue it is, for this very reason, also moot. What is politically decisive is not the complex reality, which most people do not even try to cognise, but whether the population *perceives* the current arrangement to be in its interests, and I will argue that we in general identify the interests of the population with those of the state via the concept of the nation.

My non-engagement with the economic argument is thus not merely a matter of not having time to deal with it here, or of it having already been expounded elsewhere better by others, though both are the case. In addition, I take a post-Marxist position, insofar as I think the economic question is not decisive by itself. Benefiting from imperialism economically does not automatically or straightforwardly produce fidelity to it. It can be assumed, all other things being equal, to make such loyalty more likely, but I think only because it makes it easier to convince people to believe that they should be loyal. The perception is what is decisive. The insistence of much of the left that ordinary people in the First World do not benefit from imperialism indicates precisely an attempt to manage perceptions in the opposite direction. From this point of view, my claiming that they do benefit from imperialism might seem idiotically counter-productive, but I would, with other proponents of a strong imperialist thesis, point out that the left's attempts to convince First World workers to oppose imperialism have not been very successful. As Zak Cope argues, the First World working class have been not passive but active participants in imperialism, cheerleading it and volunteering to fight in its wars, just as they have been not passive but active in fostering biopolitics.[6] This, however, does not prove that they cannot do otherwise.

We have a patriotic outlook inculcated in us that leads us to side with our state and compatriots against any foreign agency. But biopolitics produces a greater loyalty, because we have a tangible relationship to and receive things tangibly from our state that foreigners clearly do not. Biopolitics is a special, quasi-parental bond between population and state. It implies a strong and reciprocal relation of mutual interest: for most Westerners, the national interest is self-evidently our own interest, and vice versa. The individual appears in this context as a product of the nation and their survival appears dependent on that of the nation. And this is indeed no mere appearance. In our individu-ality we are actually, both cognitively and physically, produced and succoured in this national context. This does not mean, however, that we cannot or should not reject nationalism, nor that we literally cannot survive without it. It serves only to explain why modern nationalism is so fervent.

The nation is a combination of state and population forged by biopolitics. Of course, in some sense, nations existed before biopolitics. Literally, etymologically, a nation is a group of people native to the same place. But in modernity the nation is made cohesive by shared citizenship, which has increasingly diverged from the fact of birthplace. Birth in a given territory is neither necessary nor always sufficient to guarantee membership of the modern nation. The nation is today not a community of birth, but precisely a population constituted in relation to its state.

That is not to say that the nation is the only possible biopolitical combination of state and population. As Étienne Balibar argues, the association of state with nation is an historical contingency. However, it is nonetheless the case that the nation form has become the only accepted form of state in the modern era. As Balibar points out, this has led to a general perception of the nation form as natural. Nations are not natural, however. They are constituted around pre-existing geographical, linguistic, legal and cultural formations, but only with the technology of biopolitics, along with other political developments, can people with the same language and/or culture in the same geographical locus be welded into a population around a shared sense of co-nationality.

The formation of nations thus proceeded on the basis of the pre-existing realities taken up as imaginary bases for both solidary demands of the oppressed and co-ordinating action by the state. In Europe, nationalism emerged largely through popular solidarity against oppressive rulers, but was then taken up by states. A similar pattern was followed in later anti-colonial revolutions against European powers (about which more later in the book). In both cases, national solidarity is initially liberatory, but then becomes a state ideology, involving the suppression of internal dissent and difference. As Balibar suggests, there are always two moments, one racist and repressive, the other liberatory, present in all nationalisms.

1.3 Racism

In nationalism, the nation defines itself in relation to its outside. This does not in itself constitute imperialism, but nationalism and imperialism form a potent ubiquitous brew. While nationalism and imperialism are logically distinct, in practice they emerged reciprocally. The nation came into existence in the same period that Western nations were increasingly engaging in imperialist adventures. Still, imperialism exceeds the nation, and thus imperialism must produce an ideology that exceeds mere nationalism. Just as nationalism exceeds the mere patriotism that existed before the nation, so too does imperialism build on an older xenophobia to produce something similar but more acute. The specific ideology of imperialism can, I think, be identified as *racism*. The division of the population from its outside proceeds through nationalism. Imperialism requires something more than this: to actually go out and kill others, not in defence of the nation, but to take what they have, requires a justification that has historically been provided by the idea that those others are essentially different to us, members of another *race*. As Foucault observes, 'the most murderous states are also, of necessity, the most racist'.

Now, in a broad sense, xenophobia was already racism. In a narrower sense, however, racism emerges only in relation to the development of imperialism. As Foucault argues, 'Racism first develops with colonization, or in other words, with colonizing genocide. If you are functioning in the biopower mode, how can you justify the need to kill people, to kill populations, and to kill civilizations? By using the themes of evolutionism, by appealing to racism'.[7]

In point of fact, this would make racism older than nationalism, since European colonialism began in the sixteenth century. Thus, the nationalism that emerged in Europe in the nineteenth century was influenced by pre-existing imperialist racism.

Spanish colonisation in the Americas in the sixteenth century

almost immediately took the form of treating indigenous inhabitants like beasts, killing and enslaving them at will, a total
dehumanisation. This was something quite new. While massacres
were regularly conducted and all kinds of prejudices based on
appearance, behaviour, and religion circulated in the medieval
world, this did not amount to the idea that human beings were
members of distinct 'races' which gave them a particular status.[8]
Only in the fifteenth century with Africans and Amerindians did
Europeans begin to imagine other humans as akin to other
animal species. It should be noted, however, that this way of
thinking has always been shadowed by a tendency to recognise
all people's humanity. So, in the New World, the indigenous
people were slaughtered and worked to death as if their lives
were of no consequence, yet the colonisers were also keen to save
their souls by converting them to Christianity. Columbus himself
proposed enslaving all Indians, imitating and generalising the
Portuguese African slave trade, but this was not carried out,
partly because of the qualms of metropolitan authorities.
Europeans claimed that the natives were, while technically
human, absolutely lacking in any distinctively human knowl-
edges or behaviours, though this depiction also led to an opposi-
tional tendency in which they were portrayed as noble savages
lacking European corruptions.

The two tendencies, towards dehumanisation and humanism
respectively, were synthesised eventually, though not without
remainder, into the theory of races, by which other peoples were
deemed to be separate races of humanity. Linnaeus, whom
Foucault identifies as a paradigmatic classical exponent of
universal taxonomy, was in the eighteenth century the first to
classify human beings into subspecies alongside all other animals
and plants.[9]

As Francisco Bethencourt points out, thinking about race has
historically been highly diffuse and unstable; I think we can say
that this is because there is no possible objective thinking in terms

of race, and that thus racism is an unstable pseudo-scientific formation.

Dehumanisation that justified almost any treatment of non-Europeans was hegemonic in early colonisation, but was replaced, via the general abolition of slavery in the course of the nineteenth century, with a biologistic-cum-culturalist paternalism, by which colonialism came to be considered 'the white man's burden', a moral responsibility to aid 'primitive' peoples. The result has been a viscous soup of varied popular prejudices, which certainly has not yet ceased to stew.

In the metropolis, racism was formerly a relatively marginal phenomenon, important to people's feeling of superiority through membership of the chosen race, perhaps, and in making fighting in foreign wars and administering foreign colonies seem a grand enterprise. In the colonies, however, particularly for those Europeans who dwelt in them, racism was the predominant ideology. It was the undergirding logic of the status quo: the ownership of land and people's social position were decided primarily on a racial basis.

Whole nations have been established on this basis: settler societies. The US, Canada, Australia, Argentina, New Zealand, and Israel are examples of such societies, in which the indigenous inhabitants have been exterminated or extirpated and thoroughly marginalised. There are also dominant settler communities in contexts where indigenous people retain a numerical majority and have some political influence: South Africa is a case of this, as is much of Latin America, where, though in most countries in Latin America the majority are of at least partially European descent, and the divisions are less and less clear cut, elites have tended to be more ethnically European than the rest of the population.

There has been a convergence in recent decades between the racial dynamics of European countries and settler societies, as the racism of the settler group declines relatively in the latter (while remaining nonetheless entrenched), and non-European immigration to Europe has created there a burgeoning non-white underclass whose position resembles the longstanding position of non-settlers in settler societies. Racism hence tends to operate today in the same way in all First World contexts, though important differences remain; in particular, biopolitics remains more racially divided in settler societies.

One of the most brazen cases of biopolitical racism in the First World occurs in the settler state Australia. The general pattern there is an exaggerated form of one found in Western nations, of non-whites being incarcerated and killed by (predominantly white) police at much higher rates than whites, and living shorter lives in worse conditions. However, discrimination against Aboriginal people extends to a policy known as the 'NT Intervention' launched in 2007 that for the first time in decades brought back explicitly racist legislative implements, albeit only affecting the Northern Territory, an area containing the highest proportions of Aboriginal people in the country, if only a relatively small portion of the total Aboriginal populace.

A different extreme case, important not only for its uniqueness but because of the signal global importance of the society concerned, is that of the US. That nation was founded on two main racisms: one which discounted the indigenous inhabitants, allowing them to be expropriated and slaughtered, viewing them as little different from native flora and fauna; and a second, directed against Africans, allowing them to be enslaved and kept as livestock. While the first racism followed a primarily exclusionary logic, black slaves were differentially included: deliberately imported, always kept under close control in the midst of the population, but disqualified from membership of it. The inclusion-exclusion of black people I think underlies a number of unique features of American biopolitics. Perhaps the most prominent of these is the absence—at least until last year—of the universal healthcare found in other Western nations. This absence allows the exclusion of blacks from biopolitics, even though they are now formally deemed citizens with equal rights. The distinction is not absolute, of course, but tendential: 'African-Americans are 55 per cent more likely to be uninsured than white Americans'.[10] This situation represented the residue of earlier, clearer divisions. Other American exceptions I think have a similar racist dimension. One is the generally low standard of welfare and minimum employment protection in America compared to other Western nations, since black people are much more likely to be in low-wage jobs or unemployed than whites. Another is the interpretation of the right to bear arms as a right for individuals to own, and increasingly to carry and use, firearms. In most First World countries, biopolitics has decisively trumped gun ownership: allowing the population ready access to firearms is clearly at odds with protecting their health and lives. In America, however, the majority are willing to allow the risks that mass gun ownership carries, even though guns are more likely in fact to be used by gun owners on themselves, their friends, or their family than the criminals they fantasise about stopping with them. The justification for gun ownership is explicitly for the 'protection' of 'law-abiding citizens' against 'criminals'. Race is not far beneath the surface here: guns are perceived to be necessary to maintain the dividing lines within the American population; whites are disproportionately able to afford guns and obtain licences, and blacks are disproportionately in the groups guns are intended to be used against; the intention is to use guns to keep black people out, exposing them to a distributed democratic thanatopolitics. George Zimmerman's killing of Trayvon Martin is thus a paradigm of the US gun question. We may also refer her to the recently widely publicised propensity of US police to shoot black people with guns, even if they are children with toy guns, while white people are able to carry guns openly without harassment in many parts of the country.

The most spectacular case of America's biopolitical racism in recent times, however, is the aftermath of Hurricane Katrina, when black people died in their hundreds, at a mortality rate several times higher than that of whites. One can certainly suggest that the event was marked by an indifference towards the predominantly black city of New Orleans. It was also in part the fruit of the neoliberal running down of public biopolitics, with racist results. Kanye West's impromptu assessment that 'George Bush doesn't care about black people' could scarcely be more perspicuous.

Still, racist though the neglect of New Orleans was, it is not so direct as the early twentieth century massacres of hundreds of black Americans by whites in Elaine, Arkansas and Rosewood, Florida, which occurred without legal sanction, but were unpunished; similarly, in Australia, Aborigines were massacred well into the twentieth century with impunity. Piecemeal racist killings by law enforcement personnel continue to occur unpunished, but lynching is no longer tolerated. This attests to incomplete progress in extending biopolitical care, along with civil rights, to black Americans, during the last century. African Americans are today partway inside American biopolitics. Their loyalty to America is correspondingly more partial and variable than that of whites. African American political struggles focus mainly on securing entry into the biopolitical mainstream, though there remain marginal black nationalist currents which are biopolitically separatist, seeking to exit the uneven bargain of US biopolitics.

1.4 Post-Racial Racism

There are other racisms abroad in America today, doubtless with deep roots, but newly prominent. One is the vilification of Muslims, particularly during the last decade of war against Muslims overseas. Another is anti-Hispanic sentiment, driven to new heights by hysteria about mass immigration from Mexico and Central America. Each of these identifies a racial other, but via cultural rather than strictly racial features, religion in the first case, language in the second. As Balibar notes, culturalist neo-racism has displaced traditional forms of racism. Prejudices simply based on appearance are no longer acceptable in polite society, so operate in disguised conjunction with prejudices against creed and culture. Also operative here is the stigmatisation of people as 'illegal', which amounts to nothing more than the claim that they belong outside rather than inside the American population.

We are told we have today entered a 'post-racial' era, in which the explicit division on the basis of race has largely disappeared. The increasing entry of apparently non-white people into relatively privileged layers, emblematised by Obama's position as commander-in-chief of the American war machine, makes it ambiguous to what extent ethnicity continues to provide a basis for systematic exclusion. While this does not mean that white skin privilege has been done away with, or mitigate the ongoing systematic exclusion of most people of colour from positions of privilege, it does mean that race no longer operates as a clear basis for exclusion. Traditional racism survives in various forms, but has become relatively marginal as an explicit discourse; it is rather increasingly sublimated into 'dog-whistle' racism, where racism implicit in policies is explicitly denied. Of course, racism was never entirely clear-cut: since 'races' do not have an objective existence, there are intractable difficulties in identifying who should be subject to racial discrimination.

Perhaps today white privilege is more operative than racism *per se*. White people no longer directly rule much of the Third World, but still wield a preponderant influence as the executives of TNCs and the heads of imperialist First World governments. While non-whites are less actively dehumanised, white people are everywhere subtly valorised such that it is clear that places where we live are of a different type. Non-whites warrant protection by association with whites, by living in white neigh-bourhoods, attending our universities, acquiring our citizen-ships. This does not of course mean that they are entirely equal in practice.

Racism today operates in an always deniable way: white people are on average vastly wealthier and more powerful than non-whites, but look, our leader is brown; yes, the people we are killing have brown skin, but so do many of our soldiers. The same trick is played with cultural neo-racism: some of our people are also Muslims. America is not so racist that it literally kills people solely because they are of a certain race or creed; they are not Nazis. Nevertheless, people's race and creed have a statistical correlation to when they die.

The explicit standard used for making life and death decisions today is not race or creed, but citizenship. Discrimination against people according to citizenship is, in contrast to racism and cultural prejudices, deemed entirely acceptable by mainstream opinion. To say that blacks or Muslims should be deported from America is clearly racist and could not be said in polite conver-sation (though such things are still frequently said in impolite conversations, and to say it about religious groups is consid-erably more socially acceptable than to say it about racial groups). To say this about people who are not citizens by contrast remains absolutely normal; indeed, deportability has become synonymous with lacking citizenship. The fact that citizenship is largely possessed on the basis of place of birth and ancestry, and hence correlates closely to ethnicity, is seen as accidental, because it is not *solely* a matter of ethnicity.

Racism has historically provided the justification for the vastly different conditions experienced by people in the global periphery compared to the centre. Now that there are dark-skinned people in positions of influence in the centre, how can this division be made to seem acceptable to them? The answer, I would suggest, is through the myth of achievement, that is, that immigrants in the centre deserve privileges that their former compatriots do not (first and foremost perhaps because they accomplished the very difficult task of migrating in the first place). This logic, however, calls into question the current biopolitics of the centre, where much of the native population have done nothing in particular to deserve their position. It is no coincidence, I think, that the post-racial era coincides with a delegitimisation of the biopolitical care of the poor. That is, society is shifting from a race-based national biopolitics, to a micro-exclusionary form of biopolitics based on measures of desert that increasingly coincide simply with wealth. Biopolitics seems, indeed, to be increasingly subordinated to the market.

From a biopolitical point of view, class division is always racist in a broad sense, insofar as the lives of members of one class are valued differently to those of another, to the extent, for example, that there is different healthcare for the wealthy and for the poor. Doubtless, not only capitalist societies but also state socialist societies always maintained a system that was more biopolitical for some than for others. But in the current context of enormous growth in income inequality, such divisions take on a new prominence, with class actually displacing race as the key determinant of biopolitical exclusion. Historically, racism in the ordinary sense has run somewhat counter to class dynamics, producing a solidarity between workers and bosses of the same race. Today, with the decline of discrimination in employment and services, the lines between races blur, leading to the lowest section at least of the white population living among or at least at the same level as non-whites. This layer is the subject of class racism by other whites, vilified as 'white trash' in the US or 'chavs' in the UK. In the US, the prejudice against 'white trash' is effectively against white people who have fallen out of the bottom of biopolitics, and thus are in an exclusionary space. In the UK, things are different inasmuch as there is a more robust social safety net, hence the prejudice is precisely against whites who are dependent on state welfare; folk etymology has it that 'chav' is an acronym for 'council housed and violent'. Most of the British working class once inhabited council housing, but it is now the preserve of an underclass. Owen Jones' identification of chavs with 'the working class' misses the point that they are not the working class *per se*, but a lumpenproletariat. It is true, as Jones points out, that the working class have been recategorised either as chavs or as middle class, but the division here is a real one, between the employed working class and a disenfranchised welfare dependent layer. Jones, in his nostalgic enthusiasm for reconstituting the working class as such, is keen to gloss over the real divisions that have grown up in it. What Jones rightly highlights is the increasing demonisation of welfare recipients.

There are moves afoot everywhere to shunt the poorest out of biopolitics, in the name of protecting the privileges of 'ordinary taxpayers'. This tendency reached one apogee in the 2014 Australian federal budget, when it was declared that unemployed people between the ages of 25 and 30 would not be allowed to access unemployment benefits for the first six months of unemployment. The implication, though apparently missed by its architects (though fortunately not by many others), is that such people will be forced to rely on a variety of irregular methods to support themselves—family and friends, crime, and charity—or end up in hospital as a result of chronic malnutrition.

1.5 Intersectional Exclusions

Having covered race and class, one might ask about the social division that is older and more prevalent: sex. Women are certainly subjugated within biopolitics, particularly in relation to their reproductive rights. Early effects of biopolitics included reduced female mortality in childbirth, but with this came an emphasis on women's reproductive 'duty' to the nation. In the twentieth century, states have increasingly viewed population growth as more of a hazard to national well-being than a boon,

meaning women have generally been afforded greater reproductive choice. However, this imperative has notoriously led in
China to women being coerced into having fewer children. Since
our society remains patriarchal, its biopolitics does too. As
Balibar would say, we should acknowledge the historical reality
that the genealogies of imperialism, racism and nationalism all
include sexism as a prior condition of their constitution: sexism
is the deepest of all of these divisive logics. Sexism is, unlike
racism, not particularly germane to biopolitical imperialism,
since it is by and large not used to distinguish the population
from its outside; it is a distinct if ubiquitous problem and hence
will only receive treatment in passing here. Clearly there are
analogies between changes in sexism and those we have noted in
racism, however: we may posit a decline in sexism, just as there
has been a decline in racism. As with the case of racism,
prominent women in public life are pointed to as evidence that
sexism does not exist, and that women can achieve anything, and
hence sexism today increasingly takes the form of holding
individual women responsible for their own position and
ignoring systemic disadvantages.

While cataloguing exclusions of human beings, it is perhaps
pertinent to consider the exclusion of non-humans, which is
increasingly challenged. Non-human animals are clearly
excluded from biopolitics wholesale. Disease in animals is
managed by death more than by life: 10 million animals were
slaughtered as a preventative measure during the 2001 outbreak
of foot and mouth disease in the UK, for example. Certainly,
there are systematic biological attempts made in agriculture to
keep animals healthy, but these are not political. The state
mandates minimum welfare standards for animals, but the
killing of animals is, except in the case of endangered species, a
permissible alternative to keeping them alive.

Yet the rise of the idea that it is wrong to kill animals seems to
me to amount to the spilling over of the affects of biopolitics to

the non-human. The lives of pets and species owned as pets are today generally seen as sacrosanct in much of the West. Pets are frequently covered by health insurance resembling that sold to humans, and catered for by increasingly sophisticated veterinary services, although since the state doesn't guarantee these, and there's no concern for an animal population, this is not biopolitics *per se*.

What I think is interesting from our point of view is the interaction of concern for animals with biopolitical nationalism. Specifically, I am thinking of the prominent, long-running debate in Australia about the live export of animals to countries with lower animal welfare standards. The complaint is routinely made that 'Australian' animals are suffering. What is remarkable about this is that there is apparently more concern with the suffering of Australian non-human animals than the suffering of non-Australian humans in the countries under consideration. This is indeed part of a pattern, when one thinks of the luxuries and protections accorded to pets in the First World, compared with the conditions that much of humanity endure: our pets eat better and have better medical care than much of humanity.

One may also mention the extraordinary efforts made to protect certain non-human fauna of Third World countries. The protection of Third World fauna—most prominently perhaps non-human primates—is cast as an emergency demanding urgent intervention, in a way that the endangerment of First World fauna never seems to be. Species extinction in Australia, one of the few First World countries where large areas of biodiverse wilderness still exist, for example, continues apace. We can chart a highly paradoxical set of distinctions here. Hunting restrictions and the public discourse follows the logic that introduced feral animals should be exterminated and native animals protected. However, the welfare of introduced domestic animals seems to be a more significant object of concern than the well-being of native animals, with the welfare of animals kept as pets being higher than the welfare of livestock. While one might suggest an economic motive here, this scarcely makes sense. If anything, the economic imperative ought to completely elide any concern for the comfort of livestock in favour of complete instrumentalism, while pets serve no economic purpose. Rather, concern for animals seems to be in proportion to their proximity to humans. Moreover, the analogy between indifference for native animals and indifference towards native humans is glaring.

The biopolitics of First World humans continues to trump the needs of any animals: dangerous dogs are put down; attacks by sharks on humans in 2014 led the Western Australian government to cull otherwise protected animals off its coast in an attempt to make the seas safe for swimmers. The fact that there is no need for anyone to be in these seas, and indeed the fact that there is no evidence that culling sharks will actually reduce the incidence of attacks, are indicative of the extent to which the imperative to exterminate to make safe is embedded in the Australian psyche. Of course, we may say that the attempt to systematically pacify an entire landmass through the use of mechanised weaponry is a kind of logical extension of defensive killings of predators extending back to prehistory into pre-emptive action.

By contrast, when it comes to spaces in which our population does not live, different imperatives can come into play for us. As recently as the twentieth century, all the continents of the world were seen equally as composed of resources to be exploited. People, fauna, flora and land were exploitable, to be appropriated or destroyed at whim for sport and profit. Indeed, this attitude has never entirely disappeared. But it is mitigated today by new concern for ecology—which is often couched in biopolitical terms, in terms of the environment being necessary to our health and well-being, with biodiversity as a storehouse of potential genetic therapies. This logic is, however, applied primarily by the First World to the Third. Of course, conservation does occur in First World countries, but in most First World countries the valuable land has already been deforested and native megafauna exterminated, making conservation an easier gesture. In such places, our concern for animals is capable of outstripping our concerns for humans.

2

Border

When a prime minister, the political eulogist of a civic ethics, declares that France 'cannot welcome all the misery of the world', he is careful not to tell us about the criteria and the methods that will allow us to distinguish the part of the said misery that we welcome from that part which we will request—no doubt from within detention centres—to return to its place of death, so that we might continue to enjoy those unshared riches which, as we know, condition both our happiness and our 'ethics'. – Alain Badiou

The border is a condition for the possibility of biopolitical imperialism, dividing the population from its outside. That is not to say that it is necessary for biopolitics itself: one could imagine a biopolitics without borders, but that is not what we have today. Biopolitical care is rather everywhere limited to a certain territory and to certain people. This limitation is necessary but not sufficient to constitute imperialism. Biopolitical imperialism goes beyond the border as a relationship of aggression towards those outside.

I will in this chapter first sketch the emergence of a specifically biopolitical border in the twentieth century, before detailing how this border operates in an imperialistic way.

2.1 Anti-Immigrationism

We are used today to the existence of borders that control the movement of people meticulously. When we cross a national border (with some exceptions, such as within Europe's 'Schengenland'), we take for granted that our identity will be checked. One must apply in advance for permission to cross many borders in the form of a visa, making guarantees to the authorities that one will leave again. Such borders are a recent invention, however. For most of their history, borders have not been barriers to people's movement (which is not to say that people were always allowed to go wherever they wanted, only that state borders were not the way mobility was restricted). Rather, they merely defined the limit of the writ of the sovereign, and were later used to limit the movement of goods, before people themselves became the objects of containment.

The change in the function of borders to controlling flows of people relates to the development of the institution of citizenship. The category of citizen comes down to us from ancient Rome, where citizens had certain rights and responsibilities not shared by non-citizens. Free Roman men were full citizens; lesser citizenship was held by women, freedmen, and freemen of allied states, but the bulk of the population were, by contrast, slaves, without rights or citizenship. Roman citizenship differed from earlier Greek citizenship in being granted to people from outside under certain conditions.

In Medieval Europe, the absence of slavery *per se* and the rigorously hierarchical nature of society meant that the category of 'citizenship' more or less disappeared, reappearing only to describe the position of town-dwellers outside mainstream agrarian feudal society. In the Enlightenment, particularly in the American and French Revolutions that emanated from it, citizenship was reactivated as a concept.

In America, as in ancient Rome, women and slaves were excluded. Thus, existing divisions within society were redefined after American independence in terms of citizenship. Unlike in Rome, however, slavery operated on a racial basis, and American citizenship was the first in history defined in terms of race. The Naturalization Act of 1790 was passed in the second session of the first US Congress, restricting citizenship to 'free white men'. Note, it was only citizenship that was restricted, not immigration:

at this time, the idea of systematically limiting the movement of people at the border was spoken of only by philosophers— Christian Wolff and Fichte were early proponents[11]—and freedom of migration was a principle of early international law, recognised by multilateral treaties in the 1860s.[12]

American citizenship law was liberalised in the course of the nineteenth century: slavery was (after massive bloodshed) abolished, and citizenship was extended, if not yet with equal rights, to women and non-whites. From 1870, Africans could naturalise as citizens and, though other non-whites still could not, all American-born children were, regardless of race, from 1868 deemed to be Americans.

A new frontier to citizenship emerged, however, in the shape of immigration controls. In 1875, it was ruled that immigration was a federal responsibility, and the first federal immigration act, the Page Act, was passed. For the first time, power was given to US immigration officials to refuse entry to specific persons, namely Asian forced labourers and prostitutes, and to convicts from abroad. In 1882, a fee (of 50 cents) was applied to all immigrants, and a law passed banning the immigration of any Chinese who could not certify to the authorities satisfaction that they would not work as labourers. This ban lasted until 1943. This exclusion severely offended Asian nations. That problem of offensiveness was solved in part by making the exclusion mutual,[13] and therefore equal, setting the stage for the principle that people be presumed internationally immobile, and only be granted freedom to move across borders exceptionally.

Such laws closed the national territory to certain categories of human, thus preventing them in principle from ever naturalising as citizens, or from having offspring in the territory who would acquire citizenship by birth. They thus constituted a new attempt to manage the racial constitution of the American population.

The citizenry was redefined from a brotherhood of free white men, to the body of people living in America, which was then in turn itself transformed into an exclusive club with a clear average—but not absolute—ethnic and religious character, as well as a profile of health and political conservatism enforced at the border. In the course of the twentieth century, a third transformation took place, by which all explicit racism was repudiated, but through which the exclusivity of citizenship was maintained by rules of ever increasing complexity.

This same broad pattern has occurred to varying extents in all Western countries in the twentieth century. A similar but more extreme case is presented by Australia. Australia and America both began life as British colonies, on land expropriated from the native populace, harsh and forbidding places initially, which later became highly desirable destinations for Europeans, in part because of the discovery of gold, but also because of the large amount of land made available to settlers. Australia is in effect a continuity of the American experiment: it was colonised in part as an alternative destination for the deportation of British criminals once American independence meant the closure of that destination. White subjectivity in both America and Australia was profoundly racist, since the settler population's identity was established in opposition to the native. Like America's, Australia's immigration bugbear was provided by the Chinese. As in America, this began in mining districts, and led to government limiting Chinese immigration. Anti-immigration politics in America and Australia was a case of mutual incitement, with propaganda from America inflaming sentiment in Australia, while Australian colonial anti-immigration legislation set the example that the American federal government eventually followed.[14] The mining districts of California and Eastern Australia were connected by flows of people as well of ideas across the Pacific. California and the various Australian colonies sought to curtail Chinese immigration, but were all stymied in their initial efforts in the 1870s by central authority, Washington in the Californian case, London in Australia's.

Upon Australian federation in 1901, the first national Australian government made ending non-white immigration a major priority, formulating explicitly a 'White Australia Policy' that was to last for most of the century. This total closure of Australia to non-whites was a further-reaching racist policy than America ever attempted. There were moves in the direction of a 'White America' policy, but this would have required the deportation of the existing black minority who were both economically important and numerous; although there were prominent proponents of such action, and Liberia was produced as a result of some resettlement, relatively few former slaves were deported. Conversely, Australia's first prime minister cited the desire precisely to avoid an American-style 'negro problem' as a justification for preventing non-white immigration in the first place. The extant black minority in Australia was subject to a policy of either total exclusion or assimilation through mixing with the white population such that their blackness was to be 'bred out'.

White Australia was precisely a policy, rather than a law, however, unlike the earlier attempted legislation by the individual colonies that was blocked by British central authority. The principal method was a highly selective application of a 'literacy test', a method of discrimination borrowed directly from the US South, where it was used to disenfranchise black voters.

What is crucial for our purposes is that, in both cases, immigration policy was driven by popular sentiment among white men. Marxists would like to blame racism on the ruling class[15]—and indeed in its genesis they might be blameable, since it was their imperialist policies, and their propaganda for these, that created racism. But racism was then used by workers to agitate for themselves against workers of other hues. Some on the left have seen in this a strategy of the ruling class to divide and rule. If it was a strategy, it was hardly a deliberate one. There was a section of capital which, for largely economic motives, advocated labour mobility. In the opposite camp, many anti-immigration campaigners were socialists who saw immigration precisely as a tool of the bosses to drive down wages. Capital indeed did seek to import cheaper workers, and workers responded by making appeals to capitalists on a racial basis. This was possible precisely because capitalists were typically chauvinistic: the ruling class was itself also largely racist. Employers and political leaders of whites heeded white workers' racist demands because they were white themselves.

Australia at the turn of the twentieth century was at the forefront not only of racist immigration restriction but of social democratic politics worldwide. Australia's first national government of 1901 was also the first in the world to have a social democratic party in it, the Australian Labor Party (the ALP—the origins of which stretched back to 1891), albeit as the minor partner. From 1904, Labor formed the government in its own right, the first social democratic party to do so anywhere in the world. The ALP, formed out of the Australian labour movement, was racist from its inception. It was the most vociferous supporter of the White Australia Policy in 1901, demanding unsuccessfully that it expressly be embodied in legislation. The same government was one of the first national governments in the world to grant women suffrage, in 1902, but specifically only to white women—Australian Aborigines, by contrast, male or female, were not fully enfranchised until 1962. Old age pensions were established nationally by a Labor government in 1909, marking Australia's first major social welfare measure. Again, they expressly excluded '"Asiatics" (except those born in Australia) and Aboriginal natives of Australia, Africa, the Islands of the Pacific, or New Zealand'.[16] Other racist biopolitical measures followed: from 1912, a Labor government introduced a cash payment to white new mothers, intended expressly to boost the size of the white Australian population.[17]

The core component of the Labor Party's racism seems to have been the erroneous belief that non-whites undercut white wages because of lower biological requirements: Asians were believed to survive on a diet of rice, whereas white men were thought to require meat to be healthy, for example.[18] The factual basis for this concern was that Chinese workers did command lower wages. These different wage demands were based on the difference in living standards between the different parts of the world from which these workers originated, which are the basis of economic imperialism in the form of unequal exchange.

This might all seem like a monstrous aberration for a left-wing movement, but it follows a clear logic: egalitarian settler solidarity. On the goldfields of Victoria and California, the workers of the Third World and the First encountered one another directly for the first time. Previously, in European settler colonies, whites had interacted with natives who were dehumanised and subjugated, not with free workers from Asia. In the face of this other, for the first time workers of many European nations and their settler colonies encountered one another not as foreigners, but as whites: there was a free-flowing traffic from Europe to and between the diggings of South Africa, North America, and Australia.[19]

Western European states also brought in racist immigration restrictions, albeit more subtle than those found in the settler colonies. Many allowed mass immigration from Third World countries, often former colonies, during the period immediately after the Second World War, before terminating it. By contrast, the US and Australia retained barriers to such mass non-white immigration, through till 1965 in the former case and 1973 in the latter.

In Britain, to take the European example most closely related to America and Australia, immigration law and policy was never explicitly racist, though it certainly was in effect: nineteenth and early twentieth century legislation preventing permanent settlement of seamen of foreign nations was used to exclude non-white immigrants,[20] though not totally. Systematic immigration restrictions were first introduced in 1905, primarily to restrict Jewish migration from Eastern Europe,[21] though explicitly aimed only to exclude poor immigrants.

After the Second World War, in a contrary response to the incipient disintegration of the British Empire into the nebulous Commonwealth, Britain legalised unrestricted immigration from within the Commonwealth, overriding all earlier exclusions. In a context of labour shortage, the result was an unprecedented wave of immigration, mostly from Britain's then-current and former colonies in the Caribbean and South Asia. This wave ended in 1962, with the first broadside of what was to become over the next two decades an increasingly restrictive and racist immigration regime. It was once again not explicitly racist in its content, but its authors were clear about its aims. It initially restricted immigration from the Commonwealth, which included predominantly white dominions in Canada and the Antipodes equally with non-white former colonies. In respect of these white populations, however, the new regime operated very differently, since many white Commonwealth citizens had British or Irish citizenship or right of abode through descent from British colonists, or had skills that enabled them to bypass restrictions. Moreover, as Evan Smith and Marinella Marmo point out, the British government simultaneously liberalised the movement of labour to the UK for EEC citizens, who were almost all white.[22]

This new racist immigration regime was introduced primarily to pander to sizable popular opposition to immigration. Violence of working class whites against immigrants was explicitly cited as the reason for restricting immigration.[23] If there was a difference from the situation in Australia in this regard, it was that a smaller proportion of British politicians were themselves of the working class, but the effect was similar.

White workers opposed non-white immigration, I would suggest, largely because they felt it threatened their special status as citizens of the imperial power vis-à-vis the majority of humanity. The arrival of non-whites to work in the same jobs and live in the same places as whites seemed to presage in particular the removal of biopolitical protections. During the early twentieth century, biopolitics was indexed to race. Of course, there were no Nazi-style race laws in Britain, no attempt to expurgate non-Aryan elements from the population, but its biopolitics was nonetheless ethnocentric.

Lake and Reynolds point out that part of the whites-only mania in the settler colonies derived from an appreciation of the colour divide in empire, inferring that only by remaining white (or at least white-ruled) could a dominion find itself appropriately respected geopolitically. It is unclear whether this calculation was correct given the absence of a counterexample during the period, but it seems a plausible assumption given the racism of the period.

Such concerns coexisted with biologically-grounded prejudices, such as concerns about miscegenation, which in the early twentieth century—after Asian immigration had been banned and wage differentials equalised—eclipsed competition for jobs as the dominant logic of concern about the presence of Asians in California.

Both logics involved specious pseudo-biological ideas about the nature of non-whites and the effects of interbreeding, but even to the extent that they could be expressed as rational concerns about the loss of privileged status and conditions they were ill-founded. The entry of non-whites into a population has never harmed its well-being or prosperity, and white privilege itself has remained intact. Average earnings grew during the post-war wave of immigration, as did biopolitical welfare. A racial striation of society occurred, whereby many white workers departed the lowest rung of society, seen spatially in 'white flight' from the poorest neighbourhoods of the cities. This can be seen most vividly in the Northern US, where there was mass non-white migration from the South, the so-called Great

Migration, in a period in which non-white international immigration was restricted. Segregation in other countries has occurred in different ways. In France, it was accomplished by the establishment of suburban sink estates, the *banlieues*, to accommodate immigrant communities. In London, things are considerably more subtle, with poverty and affluence, black and white, exist side-by-side, not only in the same neighbourhoods, but in the same buildings. The sale of council properties institutionalised since the 1980s has resulted in housing estates in which well-to-do middle class homeowners are neighbours to impoverished council tenants. The relative lack of district-by-district segregation should not lead us to conclude that there is no race division in Britain, however. Conversely, we should not imagine these divisions are in any contemporary case absolute: everywhere in the West today non-whites are to some extent biopolitically included.

The worst fears of whites not being borne out, First World populations, now including many non-whites, ceased to be so concerned about race. They, including recent migrants and their descendants, continued to be concerned about immigration, however. While privilege no longer appears to be premised on colour, it nevertheless does seem to be premised on exclusion of others. The spectre of unrestricted labour mobility appears to threaten to reduce our wages and conditions towards levels found in other countries. First World workers have largely become satisfied that their advantage accrues not from their skin tone alone, but from their citizenship rights, and consequently have become concerned more with the sanctity of that citizenship than with the maintenance of the colour bar: anti-immigrationism has replaced racism as the hegemonic doxa; only the extreme left and libertarian right within contemporary political discourse are willing to contemplate a return to the pre-twentieth century freedom of movement of people, much as the White Australia Policy in its heyday was only challenged from these extremes.[24]

Anti-immigrationism of course retains a racist dimension, since it disproportionately targets people of colour, but this represents an inertia of racial privilege rather than a structure determined to perpetuate it. The economic value of immigrants displaces race as the primary criterion of discrimination at the border.

Former Australian Prime Minister John Howard's infamous 2001 dictum that 'we decide who comes to this country and the manner in which they come' encapsulates the ambiguities of anti-immigrationism. Specifically, it is the 'we' that is today entirely ambiguous: is it a kind of royal 'we', referring only to himself? Does it refer specifically to his administration, to his party, to his coalition, to the Australian government generically, or to the Australian people? In the case of the last, does it refer simply to the Australian citizenry as a body, or to the white Australian *ethnos* to which Howard belongs? The answer is that it refers simultaneously and ambiguously to all of these, to government and the nation, retaining an ambiguous and therefore deniable racism.

2.2 Biopolitical Borders

The territorial border has become a biopolitical border, where entry to the population is regulated, where people are checked for traces of contagion. This could be literal disease, or it could be a matter of various other characteristics deemed dangerous to the population: criminality or simply poverty.

The literal, territorial border is far from the only site where movement into the population is policed today, however. Where in the early twentieth century crossing the border was the only major obstacle to joining a population, entry has become increasingly conditional, and barriers to membership of the population proper have proliferated.

From the 1950s, 'guest worker' programmes were instituted in a number of First World countries allowing foreign workers to enter the country to work without offering a route to citizenship. In Germany, this led over several decades to the formation of a sizable, largely Turkish, multi-generational minority, entirely lacking citizenship, hence unable to vote or access civil service jobs. German citizenship law was changed subsequently to allow access to citizenship for German-born descendants of guest workers, though many have not pursued this avenue, leaving a substantial alienated non-citizen layer within the national territory, but not fully within the population.

Such stable multi-generational non-citizen groups are unusual, prevented in one way or another by citizenship law in most countries, although since the number of countries continuing to give citizenship to all persons born in their territories is dwindling, there is perhaps increasing potential for such layers to arise. Still, one finds in First World countries today large numbers of resident aliens with a variety of statuses, ranging from citizens at one end of the spectrum, to 'illegal' immigrants lacking any right to remain. In between, there are permanent residents who have almost the same rights as citizens (usually, but not always, barring certain political rights), temporary residents with a general right to work and most protections, but a maximum specified tenure in the country, and temporary workers who are allowed only to work for perhaps a single designated employer.

To give a concrete example of the complexity of modern immigration regimes, and of their biopolitical implications, I will briefly survey the Australian system, one with which I am intimately familiar as an immigrant. Here, permanent residents have most of the biopolitical rights of citizens, particularly access to health and social security (though to the latter only after a lengthy probationary period), but lack the right to vote and are barred from working in the federal public service, and can also lose their permanent residency and be expelled from the country for infractions in a way that citizens cannot. Permanent residency is in effect a necessary probationary period on the path to citizenship, minimally lasting four years, though, as its name suggests, it may be more extended than that. The multi-year ban on accessing welfare applied to permanent residents is significant: it effectively acts to prevent the indigent from remaining onshore long enough to obtain Australian citizenship. Indeed, those at risk of needing benefits and without alternative resources to call on may be denied permanent residency initially on that basis. Permanent residents are also subcategorised according to the way they gained their permanent residency initially, with some subcategories being denied access to social housing in some areas, for example.

Then there are various categories of more tenuous resident, who are shut out of some of the core Australian biopolitical structures. There are those on sponsored visas leading to permanent residency, those on sponsored work visas *not* leading to permanent residency (for example, the 457 visa), and those on 'working holiday' visas, allowing young visitors from certain First World countries to stay for one or two years, but only to work for particular employers for defined periods within that time. Then there are student visas, allowing students to live and work part-time in Australia, with an end date tied to the end of their studies, and tourist visas, with short expiries, entitling visitors to nothing beyond reciprocal healthcare during a brief visit. Each of these categories are shut out of some welfare services. Lastly, as in any country, there are illegal immigrants, who have the fewest rights.

Through these categories, a series of 'biopolitical borders' is set up around various forms of care, with full citizens generally allowed full access, and others restricted.[25] In Australia, to continue with this example, healthcare depends on visa status: residents temporary and permanent get the same healthcare entitlements as citizens; students are required to have private health insurance that substitutes for this; visitors from many countries get emergency care through reciprocal arrangements, but others are left having to pay. By contrast, in the UK, healthcare access is entirely unregulated in emergency cases i.e. all will be seen, legal or not—and general medical care is regulated only by having to prove one's factual residence in the area, not its legitimacy. In the US, of course, there is a highly varied access to healthcare within a largely for-profit medical sector.

Such variation in access to services, however it is organised in a given country, constitutes a sophisticated control mechanism. It sets up a series of hoops that must be jumped through in order to gain entry to the population, and limits the exposure of the population to those who might be biological or economic risks, while allowing it to benefit from their presence. This regime is always messy, blurred in places and vulnerable to fraud, but it nonetheless functions. The border serves to protect, to divide, to create incentives, to ensure the maintenance of biopolitics through gradated access.

It operates even—or indeed especially—where it might appear to have failed, that is, through 'illegal' immigration. The illegality of immigrants requires them to remain invisible, compliant, uncomplaining, because the cost of becoming visible to the authorities is worse than quitting their job: it means losing their job plus deportation. In some countries, such as the US and Australia, incarceration must be added to this list of penalties. Something similar may be said about legal workers on restrictive visas: student visas restrict the hours that students can work, while high student fees force them to work longer hours, pushing them to work outside of legal protections; temporary work visas specifically strip workers of biopolitical and labour rights, and make them beholden to their employer for their right to remain in the country, leading them to accept illegal ill-treatment by their employers rather than risk complaining. Such immigrants could be categorised as 'partially legal' and as such their predicament has many of the same features as that of illegal immigrants, albeit in a lesser form.

There are sizable economic interests vested in keeping 'illegal'—and therefore cheap and expendable—labour flowing as such. The demand to limit immigration, and the demand for cheap, subordinate labour, are mutually complementary within the emergent strategy of immigration control: measures ostensibly designed to keep immigrants out in fact serve to ensure that those immigrants who circumvent them are cut out of costly biopolitical and employment protections, forming a layer of cheap labour partly outside of the biopolitics of the population. Anti-immigrationists keep complaining about immigration, the efforts to deport people are stepped up, and immigrants are harassed, scared, put in their place. The net result of policies aimed at deportation is for those immigrants not deported to licence their harassment and oppression *in situ*. This is not to say that immigration law is simply a trick—it is, rather, part of an emergent strategy involving a compromise between different forces.

Deportation policies accentuate existing imperialist dynamics. Deportation can be applied to non-citizen but legally resident aliens if they commit crimes, further filtering the population, and indeed, although in principle applicable to all undocumented migrants, is far more likely to be applied to the indigent and criminals, and to the simply poor, than others who can better evade detection by authorities. The horrifying results of the process of mass deportation of criminals has in recent years been seen in Central America, resulting in an effective deportation of organised gang warfare from American cities to countries already destroyed by years of US-sponsored civil war.[26]

Anti-'illegal' discrimination spills over by association of cultural and ethnic characteristics to others from the same ethnic background with 'legal' status, thus providing a jurisprudential basis for racism against, for example, Hispanic people in the US. This builds on a longer history of the racist exclusion of Hispanics in America. This too is part of the strategy: endemic racism continues to be part of the enforcement and justification of biopolitical borders, even if, as I argue, the general move is away from racism and towards a meritocratic moralism, which is, in effect, class racism.

For a different example of this general effect of compromise in forming strategy, one can look at the use of borders to control the spread of disease. Australia enforces a 'health requirement' for many visas, which explicitly seeks to 'minimise health risks' to the Australian population and to 'contain public expenditure on health' (i.e. by excluding people with health conditions that would be expensive to treat). The diseases screened for under this requirement are tuberculosis, hepatitis, and HIV.

Now, from the point of view of preventing infectious disease, the optimal scenario would be to close the border completely. Australia and other island states could practicably do this. Not only do they not do it, however, but they do not screen short-term visitors for diseases at all. This is an obvious concession to practicality, and to economics. Specifically, tourism and business require people to be able to visit the country at short notice without medical checks. The Australian state attempts therefore only to prevent itself being responsible for caring for people with expensive diseases, not seriously to prevent the spread of disease.

An attempt rigorously to exclude HIV from a population was made by Cuba, but only once the virus was already in the territory, by quarantining all sufferers.[27] During this period Cuba was experiencing negligible immigration, and relatively little movement of people even on a temporary basis. Despite the obvious problems such a policy faces, namely that HIV does not manifest itself until months after exposure so testing gives many false negatives, and that people with the disease are incentivised by such a policy to conceal their status in order to avoid quarantine, it nonetheless significantly slowed the rate of infection, but was abandoned, ostensibly for economic reasons.

In both cases, it seems biopolitical motives are subordinated to economic ones. However, one must remember the extent to which biopolitics itself depends on economics: economic prosperity enables biopolitics. The negative economic consequences of border closure thus have the potential to damage the population as much as disease. Still, non-biopolitical considerations contribute to the profusion of immigration categories, shaping our biopolitics. The net effect is an increasing striation of biopolitics within the national territory.

2.3 World Borders

Some see in the exclusion of immigrants already inside a country from its population the creation of an 'internal Third World' within the First. Hardt and Negri conclude from this and the existence of wealthy enclaves in poor countries that the distinction between the Third and First Worlds is no more. I disagree. Those who dwell in the midst of the First World without protection have escaped the Third World, although they find the fullness of the First denied to them. They are not part of First World populations, but by being in First World territory benefit from the background biopolitics of the place: from relative safety from violence perhaps, from relatively high-paying (albeit illegal) work, from emergency medical care, from cleanliness and absence of endemic disease. Only those trafficked into domestic or sexual slavery could perhaps be said not to benefit at all from their migration.

The boundary between Third and First World holds relatively firm in contrast to boundaries within the each of the two Worlds. Within the Third World, territorial borders are close to moot when it comes to migration: the borders between most Third World countries are large land borders with minimal policing, and there is little enforcement of immigration restrictions within the national territory (although the restrictions may officially be quite onerous). More importantly, for our purposes, the kind of biopolitical services to which access might be denied on the basis of immigration status are relatively insignificant in the poorest countries. That is not to say that they are entirely absent, however, and they are vital for those who depend on them. Several intra-First World borders have also been deliberately loosened: intra-European borders in particular have more or less been abolished as impediments to the movement of people, though barriers to accessing biopolitical services inside countries are more intractable.

By contrast, First World-Third World interfaces are heavily policed. There are two main ones: the US-Mexican border and the Mediterranean. Much of the former's almost 2,000 miles are relatively remote desert, itself constituting a significant and often lethal obstacle. There has been much tough talk in the last decade of a wall and patrols, and there have been decades of vigilantism. These measures have significantly reduced illegal cross-border traffic, though the flows remain sizable.

The Mediterranean crossing is a greater obstacle. African migrants must first cross the Sahara desert before reaching the sea, itself a serious obstacle for poor people. The cost of life in the combined crossing is enormous, but a steady flow nonetheless lands on the coastlines in Spain, Italy, Greece, and on Malta. The economy of Western Europe has lately relied much less than the US on illegal Third World immigrant labour, because the expansion of the EU eastward into the old Second World has opened up a great reservoir of legal cheap labour, though agriculture in Spain and Italy in particular continues to rely on the even cheaper illegal labour of Africans.

There are more minor interfaces, such as the Timor Sea between Indonesia and Australia, notable for its relative impass-ability and the extreme measures adopted by the Australian state to prevent irregular movement across it into Australia. Australia is naturally more difficult to enter than any other First World nation since it is proverbially 'girt by sea' and, even if one can cross this sea, one lands on inhospitable coasts, thousands of kilometres of desert from major habitations. Thus the irregular flows so prominent in most other First World countries are absent in Australia. Those who come by boat are mostly asylum-seekers actively seeking interception by Australian authorities rather than attempting surreptitiously to enter the country. Illegal immigrants in Australia are almost all people who enter the country legally and then 'overstay' their visa.

Most of the First World is much more accessible to people from the Third World than Australia is. The most direct inter-faces are found in Palestine and South Africa, where the division between First and Third occurs within countries. While in South Africa, populations were formerly formally separated within the same country, today there is officially one population, but white and black continue to exist largely in distinct worlds, with the stark division between the private and public healthcare systems, for example, facilitating this. In Israel, the formal separation remains, albeit striated: the Israeli citizenry are separated from the largely dispossessed Palestinian population corralled in the occupied territories, and indeed Gaza has been separated from the West Bank, and the latter carved into discontinuous enclaves, while within Israel proper non-Jewish citizens have an unofficially inferior status to Jewish citizens, through discrimination in the use of funds for—and use of violence against—Arab citizens.

Not dissimilarly, in places on the American land border with Mexico, towns on either side of the border exist in two worlds separated only by metres—and prodigious fortifications.

The great interworld borders constitute the primary infra-structure of global apartheid, excluding most people. Only a small portion of the people of the Third World are deemed acceptable, through onerous bureaucratic assessments, to enter the First World without circumventing these, based on the application of economic and biopolitical criteria. The border operates as a selectively permeable membrane, allowing in elements advantageous to the population.

3

Traffic

If the free-traders cannot understand how one nation can grow rich at the expense of another, we need not wonder, since these same gentlemen also refuse to understand how within one country one class can enrich itself at the expense of another. – Karl Marx

3.1 Demographic Incline

In the previous chapter, imperialism was relatively absent as a theme: I only detailed the way in which people are excluded from the First World's biopolitics. Yet the immigration regime is not just exclusionary, but actively biopolitically imperialist: it works to enhance the populations of the First World at the expense of those outside.

Not only do immigration controls allow only the most desirable immigrants to cross the border into the population, but nations and corporations mount active campaigns to attract the most desirable potential citizens and workers from outside. The effect of this is simple, stark, and sizeable: the most vital, the most skilled, the wealthiest people in the Third World are drawn into the First. Today's legal migrants are on average wealthier, healthier and more skilled than the existing First World average, improving the First World population's demographic profile, making it younger and more educated, while at the same time having the diametrically opposite effect on the demographic profile of the countries these migrants come from, rendering them older, sicker, less skilled, more ignorant. Immigrants, legal or illegal, burden the state much less than the average resident, illegal immigrants because they are not given access to the requisite services and legal immigrants because they are selected for their unlikeliness to require state services.

A paradigmatic case, and one which is particularly biopolitically devastating, is the migration of skilled medical personnel. There is an international pyramid of medical migration, whereby Third World doctors and nurses migrate to First World countries, such as Britain, which have perennial shortages of such workers, then, in turn, First World medics migrate towards the richest countries, particularly towards the US, where the private medical system allows doctors in particular to command exaggerated remuneration. The net result is entire Third World countries without medical specialists in a range of areas. To put things starkly, people in the Third World are dying so that Americans may live longer, healthier lives.

Most migrants are of course less skilled than doctors, but even in the case of unskilled migrants, demographic imperialism is operative. Even they have a generally desirable demographic profile, both relative to the population they come from and to the one they are entering, being relatively young, enterprising, wealthy, educated. This is true even of irregular 'illegal' migrants—one must be resourceful as well as desperate to elude the barriers to entering the First World. Much as the Middle Passage involved a brutal selection of the healthiest slaves by placing them in inhuman conditions where a large proportion perished, the obstacles to crossing into the First World—the desert border of Mexico and the US, or the Sahara and Mediterranean crossing—kill many, selecting out the hardiest, who receive no compensation for their ordeal other than simply the privilege of existing tenuously in the First World.

As is often noted in the public discourse these days, most First World countries are undergoing a demographic decline, with an ageing population reproducing below the replacement rate. Even relatively unskilled immigrants fill this gap, both economically by filling menial necessary positions lacking local aspirants, and demographically, by providing the missing future population.

This constitutes an effective offshoring of reproduction and education. Rather than pay benefits or wages to workers locally to produce children, which is expensive given the cost of medical care, education, housing, food and entertainment in First World countries, one can simply import ready-made young adults from poor countries where the cost of producing them is low. In doing so, the best and brightest products of systems of education and healthcare that have bad overall outcomes are plucked out: highly competent and healthy individuals are low-cost to the imperialist country partly because it does not need to absorb the detritus of sick and ignorant individuals produced by inadequate medical and educational systems.

Traffic in people to provide unskilled labour to fill the gap in the First World's dwindling labour supply does not generally have the negative impact on the Third World of causing a shortage of unskilled labour. It does, however, contribute to the skills shortage in the Third World, since many of those who migrate from the Third World to perform unskilled labour in the First are either themselves skilled, or could have used the initiative and energy they employ in getting to the First World otherwise in acquiring skills or starting businesses in the Third World. This is true even of workers who are specifically allowed entry to the First World based on a skill set that is supposedly required by the destination economy. Skilled immigration categories allow immigration by skilled workers who, for a variety of reasons (lack of local recognition of qualifications, lack of language skills, racism, lack of connections), end up working in other jobs. For example, engineers from India migrate to Australia to drive taxis.

This kind of migration is surely devastating to the source countries, without being correspondingly beneficial to First World society, though it does have advantages for the latter. From the First World point of view, even if a taxi driver without an engineering degree would drive the taxi just as well, they might as well have the engineer. Firstly, it means those skills are there in case they are needed, and secondly, the likelihood is that the progeny of these imported highly educated workers will themselves attain high educational levels. One might also suggest that the damage this immigration does to the Third World is a benefit, since it reduces the Third World source country's potential to compete economically.

One might argue that the remittances that migrants send back compensate countries of origin, but in fact remittances are biopolitically damaging. They inhibit the development of local economies, fostering dependency by entire communities on First World economies, in a similar way to the case of development 'aid' that I will discuss in the next chapter. People in African villages quite rationally pool all their resources in an effort to send their favoured sons North to prosperity, to countries where even the most menial and tenuous jobs can yield extraordinary wealth by Third World standards.

The First World doesn't even need to expend effort to recruit people from the Third World (though it does sometimes actively recruit, anxious to attract the best possible migrants and to outcompete other rich countries): they willingly apply. The First World can actually make migrants pay for the privilege of migrating. To come to the West legally, one can be expected to spend tens of thousands of dollars in immigration fees and expenses, commonly also taking an (often practically unnecessary) educational course over several years to qualify to apply for residency. Both of these services are liable to be priced over the cost of delivery, that is, to be profitable for the destination country.

3.2 Offshoring

So skilled and unskilled workers are drawn into the First World to build it up. There is also a trade in individuals for the construction of families by First World citizens, a trade in women and children in particular. Citizens of the First World can today source spouses—so-called 'mail order brides'—or children from Third World countries, constituting another brake on the demographic decline of our populations (there is a similar trend today in China and South Korea, redressing the gender imbalance in these countries by importing women from poorer East Asian countries, particularly Vietnam). A growing alternative to the booming adoption trade is the emerging practice of using Third World wombs to grow one's own biological progeny in surrogacy arrangements, about which more soon.

The offshoring of the production of life is resisted by conservatives who prefer the 'traditional' pattern of women devoting themselves to bearing and rearing children. Most Western states subsidise onshore reproduction through the provision of benefits. These of course are meant primarily as a form of biopolitical care for parents and children, rather than an active inducement to breed, but conservative support is premised to a large extent on nationalist natalism, and indeed ultimately on racism: several states offer pointed inducements to parents to reproduce in order to stem the demographic decline of the nation—but since this demographic decline could be more cheaply staunched by freer immigration, it is actually only the decline of the ethnic group that this addresses.

Adoption from and surrogacy in the Third World is a biopolitical colonisation of subaltern bodies, but it is not biopolitical imperialism in our sense, because it causes negligible damage to the populations concerned, even if it often traumatises individuals. Nevertheless, it is a visceral example of the myriad ways in which First World biopolitics is facilitated by or dependent on the poverty of the Third World.

The biopolitically imperialist aspect of surrogacy and the adoption trade lies in the further diversion of the medical resources of Third World countries towards First World uses. In this respect it is simply another form of 'medical tourism': when

First Worlders travel to Third World countries for medical procedures, they tie up the residual personnel who have not already migrated to the First World. An interesting, nascent, form of this, converse to adoption and surrogacy, is the trend to ship the First World elderly offshore to spend their declining years in cheap foreign nursing homes. This does not excise them from the First World population—it is merely a bid to save money—but it does neatly mitigate the problem of the aging of the population. While this is today more deliberate than in the past, it has been happening for decades through the choices of elders to retire to cheaper locales. One day perhaps death might be largely banished to the Third World. Like 'offshoring' in general, this involves tying up sparse skilled Third World labour in catering to First World citizens instead of their compatriots.

The offshoring of elder care and importation of care workers are merely direct cases of a broader effect created by the financialisation of First World retirement. With increased longevity and lower birth rates, we are told that greater savings rates must be achieved to pay for retirement. These savings are essentially intended to pay for young people to do the work required by retired people in the future. What this translates into is a storing up of various kinds of wealth to be selectively released to the young as an inducement for them to do this labour.

If our societies were hermetically sealed, this would amount to a restructuring of society with a greater proportion of labour going to the needs of the elderly. Since retirement savings of First World workers are globalised, however, our retirement planning passes through the circuits of imperialism. As the First World ages, it will work less, rely on its investments and unequal exchange to keep it alive, to feed it, to treat its ailments. We expect the slack to be taken up by the expansive youth of the Third World. By immigration they will replenish the First World, by their labour in the Third World they will provide the goods and profits to pay for our care.

This might seem like a good bargain for all concerned: jobs for the people of the Third World, care for the First World's old people. The problem is that it is premised on imperialist power and ownership structures: retirement funds are invested in imperialist concerns which reap superprofits from the Third World and then use these superprofits to hire people from the Third World at knock-down rates. This situation is exploitative and hence requires the threat of force to keep going.

Public pensions too may be said to depend on imperialism to the extent that biopolitics is imperialist anyway, but the financialisation of pensions into the private sector goes further. Where previously old age pensions were mostly paid out of tax receipts, today they are increasingly tradeable financial products, with elder care paid for by the performance of investments by pension funds. One explicit purpose of this is to circumvent the problem of demographic decline by making retirement incomes contingent not on national product but on the performance of globalised investments. The great collective savings of First World workers can be expected to interact with the many young people in the Third World entirely without savings who must work to get money to in effect make First World pensioners the exploiters of the global poor.

3.3 Trading Health

Not only people but parts of their bodies—organs, hair, and fluids—are increasingly traded separately across borders.

The sale of human hair on a massive scale from poor women to rich ones in other parts of the world is emblematic, but not biopolitically damaging, not least since hair is dead tissue anyway, though it is yet another example of the price advantage to First World consumers of Third World poverty—how much would wigs of human hair cost if everyone in the world had our living standards?

The sale of organs is, by contrast, the most visceral possible case of biopolitical imperialism, since it damages the health of the donor. The literal ripping of parts from poor people's bodies to go inside rich people represents a situation in which someone's organic composition has become their most significant moveable asset, worth more than their labour power. While there are relatively few organic components that one can sell without dying, it is possible to sacrifice one's entire body in order to obtain money posthumously for one's family—and there are also cases where organs are harvested from non-consenting bodies. Even kidney removal, though it does not directly kill you to lose one, can have disastrous consequences: it leads to clear declines in both health and income among kidney donors, who are paid on average a little over a thousand dollars per organ.[28]

Organ trafficking is illegal in much of the First World, banned, for example, inside the EU, but travel by citizens to buy organs in other countries is not.[29] Only Germany (which continues for historic reasons to be peculiarly sensitive to such bioethical concerns) has criminalised such travel, but this is scarcely enforceable.

There is also trade in other products and components of human bodies, for example, in human ova. Donna Dickenson details a trade from Southern and Eastern European women to Northwestern European women, with some women in the former regions becoming professional ova donors.[30] Dickenson suggests this is actively harmful to donor health, specifically because of the hormones used to stimulate ovulation.[31]

Another way in which Third World bodies are used for medical purposes is *in situ* as test subjects for drugs not yet approved for Western patients.[32] As well as putting people at risk by using drugs on them not deemed safe for First World bodies, such trials once again replicate the standard problems of offshoring, taking facilities and personnel away from the local healthcare apparatus to do the testing. Unlike organ donors, these test subjects are not even remunerated.

There is even a negative version of this, the use of Third World people as placebo control groups where effective treatments exist. The denial of available, approved drugs to Third World people, while resources are expended monitoring them, in effect turns their very biopolitical marginalisation into an exploitable resource.[33]

Standard 'ethical' objections to such treatment ignore the systematic nature of this discrimination. The headline grabbing scandals—testing, organ sales, surrogacy—are merely the most visceral manifestations of biopolitical imperialism. Everyday unequal exchange already represents lower health and safety conditions than would be allowed in the First World, allowing Third World workers to be maimed and killed at a greater rate. Extreme cases in point include the export of toxic waste to the Third World, the children living in waste piles scavenging for scrap metal, the Chinese workers sifting mercury out of circuit boards without respirators.

We must also note the scandal of drug pricing and the aggressive attempts by Western companies and Western governments on their behalf to prevent the production of generic drugs (the US government, for example, actively tried to prevent the South African government declaring a state of emergency in relation to AIDS, which would have allowed it to circumvent WTO rules preventing use of generic antiretrovirals).[34] People are allowed to die for the sake of Western drug companies' profits. This does not, contrary to the companies' claims, stimulate the production of new drugs, but it is a boon for First World economies, where most drug patents are held.

3.4 Refugees

The great exception to the imperialistic pattern in migration policy might appear to be the First World's reception of asylum-seekers. They are not selected for their demographic desirability—they are rather allowed in precisely because their condition is abject. Yet, it must be noted that the asylum-seekers who reach Western nations are on average not the most abject of their countrymen. The great mass of refugees from Third World countries flees from one Third World country to another. Asylum-seekers who flee to the First World either do so through official channels or through direct travel to the destination country, which are both in their own ways difficult to navigate successfully.

Indeed, asylum-seekers are the tip of an iceberg of misery. The right employ this fact to oppose accepting them: on the one hand they are vilified as wealthy scroungers, on the other as a leak in a dyke holding back a flood of humanity—if we allow in a trickle, the walls may break. The left say to this, quite plausibly: no, we can allow in a limited number, properly regulated, a steady, permanent trickle of refugees from the horror of the rest of the world; we can bring them in, and turn them to our advantage.

The contemporary legal status of the refugee derives from the Convention relating to the Status of Refugees, established in 1951 to deal with the problem of displaced persons in Europe after the Second World War. It was extended in 1967 to cover all people worldwide, in a protocol that all First World nations are party to. The convention builds on the older customary principle of non-refoulement, that states should not send people back to a place where they would be persecuted.

This framework enshrines a division between the politically persecuted and the merely wretched. The perverse unintended consequence of this is that political persecution constitutes a route to escape poverty, indeed incentivising people to cast themselves as persecuted. While political persecution can entail an imminent risk of death and punishment, many in the Third World live in danger of death and misery not arising from political persecution and hence lack grounds for asylum.

In this way, the refugee regime is essentially elitist, resting on a distinction between the needs of political intellectuals and the needs of hungry peasants, by which the former are deemed worthy and the latter not. Yet to be tortured with electric shocks is not obviously less pleasant than to watch one's children die from malnutrition. And imperialism may be implicated in both.

The refugee question is so vexed in part because it is the point at which the whole structure of international exclusion threatens to crumble. When refugees seek asylum within our borders, their misery comes into direct contrast with our privilege. What happens at this point is telling. All strands of mainstream political opinion in the First World understand our privilege as essentially autochthonous, which is to say, as earned and deserved by us. A philosophical elaboration of this position is found in the thought of John Rawls, in which the difference between poor and rich countries, between tyrannies and liberal democracies, is primarily interpreted as a difference of 'national savings' caused by profligacy and frugality respectively (was there ever a more Protestant political theory?). First World opinion then divides into those who are willing to be relatively 'generous' with their hospitality and those who refuse it. Since the category of refugee under the Refugee Convention is clearly containable within our existing biopolitics, the stance that the state and population take on this question is relatively inconsequential.

Whence then the extraordinary vilification of refugees in some countries? The most extreme example of this today is, once again, Australia, where refugees represent almost the only irregular flow of human beings, and hence occupy the position occupied by illegal immigrants in the public discourse in other jurisdictions, but anti-asylum seeker sentiment has run high in other First World countries. It is worth noting that refugees are almost always a minority of total immigration, but tend to be a lightning rod for opprobrium because they are the most threatening type of immigrants: people who come not because they are selected by the recipient nation, nor because they want to work, but because they did not fit in where they came from. Traumatised and in need of assistance, refugees have peculiar difficulty adapting to their new situation. They tend to be more likely than the average for the host population to require biopolitical care—the opposite to the situation of most immigrants. Refugees may thus be granted preferential access to services such as housing—which of course they are likely to need much more desperately than most applicants. This nonetheless draws hostility within the host country from those who perceive themselves as competing for the same services and from those who perceive themselves as paying for them. In a climate of anti-immigrationism and racism, persecuting refugees has proven a politically profitable move in several countries, though it is carefully cast in humanitarian and indeed biopolitical terms: mistreatment of refugees is characterised as necessary to attack the 'inhuman' industry of 'people smuggling', to protect the very people it persecutes by deterring them from embarking on dangerous journeys. Since refugees are of more ambiguous benefit to the recipient society than other forms of migrant, vilifying them provides a scapegoat for racist sentiment without curtailing useful flows of economic migration.

Conversely, the peculiar horror expressed in Australia for example by many at the treatment of refugees by the Australian government can be construed as due to the liminal situation of refugees in relation to the Australian territory and population. While the government is adamant on keeping these refugees out of both the Australian territory and its population, they can act only once refugees have entered Australian territorial waters, and hence Australian jurisdiction. Refugees then end up held in concentration camps in Australian territory, or more recently outside Australia, but with Australian guards, under Australian authority. This suspension of biopolitics by and within Australia is indeed confronting to any who desire to protect the universality of Australian biopolitics—if such things are allowed to happen today to refugees, tomorrow they will perhaps be done to some other group. The objection to sending refugees to third countries after their asylum applications are assessed follows a similar logic—who might be exiled next?

There is one form of refugee migration which is of great positive importance to the host polity, namely the harbouring of dissidents from hostile states. Political dissidents from anti-imperialist states are taken in by Western nations, where they set up base and work to destabilise the governments that persecuted them. Such dissidents can constitute embryonic future pro-Western governments. We may also refer to a marginal, but not insignificant and quite important phenomenon, by which the West takes in refugees persecuted by repressive regimes it supports, thus creating a release-valve for pressure in those societies. For example, the extraordinarily homophobic current regime in Honduras, installed in a US-backed coup in 2009, is supported by the US while it also fast-tracks asylum applications by LGBT people fleeing the country. This primarily serves the function of alleviating pressure on the US government not to support the Honduran regime.[35]

3.5 Land and Food

Thus far in this chapter we have dealt with traffic of life from the Third World to the First, specific trades involving bodies and organs. Another organic trade that has biopolitical ramifications is that in food. The problem here is simply that the First World wants the Third World's food, but the Third World needs it to live. Since food is a globalised commodity, it is easy for the First World to take food from the Third, and not obvious when it is happening.

There are several ways in which the First World takes food out of the mouths of the poorest people: 1) Specific food products consumed by people in the Third World are targeted for export to the First World; 2) Land used to grow food in the

Third World is acquired by foreign interests to grow crops ('cash crops') for export; and 3) Land in the First World used to grow food consumed in the Third World is repurposed for First World use.

Although 1) would seem to be the most obvious form of food theft, it is relatively rare. A dwindling majority of the people of the Third World continues to live hand-to-mouth from the land through subsistence agriculture, and they will not sell the food they need. A recent instance of a specific targeting of a Third World staple, however, is the craze in the West for the traditional Andean grain quinoa, which has become fashionable in the West, and has thus suddenly been priced beyond the means of locals who have long relied on it as a staple.[36] The great paradox of this is that quinoa is prized in the West for containing an extraordinary range of nutrients – something hardly required by Westerners with access to an array of different sources of these, but vital to its traditional consumers. A similar fate has befallen the seeds of the Indian neem tree, an age-old pharmaceutical product of diverse uses, now a cash crop not available for local use.[37]

The direct acquisition of land is by contrast a more important recent trend, a form of enclosure, expropriating smallholders. Fuelled by concerns about food availability in the likely event of future environmental collapse and increasing worldwide demand for food, arable land throughout the world has become a hot investment, with everyone from American universities to Gulf Arab regimes buying it up. The perverse effect of this is to move towards a situation where poor and hungry regions provide food to rich ones. As a general phenomenon, this is at least as old as colonialism. Cash crops like coffee have long been grown in the Third World, taking up land and resources that might otherwise be used to grow food for local use, first on colonial plantations, later to service debt obligations to First World banks. Millions of Indians died under British domination in the nineteenth century solely because they could not afford food, due to the exportation of food to the metropole.[38]

Domination of food supply is no small component of imperialism. Settlers' seizure of vast areas of arable land—particularly in North America—from indigenous peoples has allowed settler colonies to produce massive food surpluses that make them the 'bread basket of the world', and make many areas of the world dependent on its exports. It regularly waves the stick of cutting off food supplies to coerce nations to toe its line, for example with Iraq during the 1990s with devastating consequences, about which more in Chapter 5. The enormous government subsidies paid in the US—and indeed almost everywhere else in the First World—to farmers must be understood in this context.

This leads us to our third problem, the repurposing of First World agricultural production: since the world is dependent, through world food markets, on food produced in the First World, reducing First World food production raises prices and kills poor people in the Third World. A recent example of this is the production of biofuel ethanol, with food (primarily maize) directly turned into fuel in an effort to reduce carbon dioxide emissions. This was credited by itself with causing a significant food price crisis in the last decade. Here, what little climate action we see by wealthy states is at the expense of the world's poor.

Any reduction of food production can be presumed to have similar effects. Thus, the building of housing on arable land in either the First World, or the conversion of land use from basic foodstuffs to luxury products, including meat, which require more land to produce the same amount of food energy, will harm the masses of people in the Third World whose lives are dependent on the prices of staples traded in a global marketplace.

The irony is that the First World is consuming too much food per capita, in the sense that its overeating is making it sick, producing the much touted 'obesity epidemic'. This seems to contradict the thesis of biopolitical imperialism, since the West's behaviour is actually harming its populations, as well as the Third World's. Biopolitics asserts itself, however, in the public health discourse, with so many wringing their hands over obesity. This debate occurs entirely within the strategy of imperialism, moreover, with the proceeds of imperialism fattening people, and the attempts at a solution passing inevitably through the circuits of imperialism. The way the obesity problem is addressed is by encouraging people to eat a healthier diet, more fresh produce, more vegetables, which are more expensive to produce. A healthy diet means eating much more to get one's caloric requirement than is supplied by a dangerously unhealthy diet of processed sugars and starches. More than anything, it is maize in its processed forms that drives obesity in its heartland, the US. Maize is a prodigious crop, producing more calories per hectare than any other, with other staple cereals rice and wheat coming a close second and third.[39] It should be said moreover that, at present, the greatest waste is not the new uses of food crops, either the conversion to ethanol or the growing of healthful crops instead, but the conversion of cereal grains to meat. This has almost nothing to do with health—consumption of fatty meats is another major driver of obesity and a killer—and almost everything to do with imperialism, inasmuch as it is a matter of producing a completely unnecessary and expensive food product to meet the preferences of First World consumers. The point is, though, that the touted alternative, pushed through the dual biopolitical demands for healthier citizens and the protection of animals, is as imperialist as the old one: the First World is enjoined to consume more, not less, of the world's resources, growing crops that require more resources, growing less intensively through organic farming. We are regularly enjoined to eat more fish for health too, in the context of existing consumption of fish which is chronically unsustainable, with supertrawlers scouring the world's oceans with little to no discrimination to provide food to the highest bidder, which means, of course, us. In West Africa, in particular, European industrialised fishing is helping to destroy the local traditional source of subsistence.[40]

4

Aid

> Accordingly, with admirable, though misdirected intentions, they very seriously and very sentimentally set themselves to the task of remedying the evils that they see. But their remedies do not cure the disease: they merely prolong it. Indeed, their remedies are part of the disease. – Oscar Wilde

In the previous chapter, we dealt with flows from Third World to First. In this chapter, we will deal with flows in the opposite direction, principally with what is called 'aid'. Aid comprises money and material, accompanied only in a limited and for the most part temporary way by personnel. It seems to be characterisable largely as one of many economic flows, then.

The pattern of economic flows has long been inimical to the Third World. Suffering the 'Lucas Paradox', it has historically attracted little investment. Burdened with massive debts, the balance of its economic flows has tended to be strongly outward. This is so even excluding the extent to which trade is unequal exchange to the advantage of the First World, such that the formal valuation of its exports relative to the value of what it imports misrepresents the cost of production.

Exceptions to this pattern abound, however, and recently the pattern has been rather different. The current pattern is for Third World economies that are growing rapidly to export capital, whereas ones that aren't are now major importers. On average, the poorer a country is, the greater the percentage of its GDP is composed by inflowing capital, and the greater the proportion of this inflow is composed of aid.

Now, this might seem like a desirable pattern, that poor countries need this money to develop. However, foreign direct investment and loans both have obvious drawbacks: loans must be repaid with interest, and investors are seeking a return, that is, are predatory and exploitative. While such flows can be an overall boon, they often are not. Investment is not about biopolitics—it's about commercial interests that may care for their own workers but won't invest in the broader economy unless they are forced to. Loans may be used to pay for biopolitical infrastructure, but create indebtedness, and in recent decades have been made conditional on actively destroying biopolitics, which has been seen as a brake on economic development because of the portion of GDP tied up in paying for it.

Aid, by contrast, would seem to be an unmitigated bonus: one might imagine that aid is essentially free, coming without strings attached. This is not true, however. Most of what is classified as First World 'aid' to the Third World is actually composed of development loans. Moreover, even where aid is not explicitly conditional, there is often some diplomatic or economic quid pro quo expected. The typical image of aid, propagated by NGOs in their appeals for funding from the First World public, actually represents only a small sector of aid. I will argue, however, that even aid that is entirely gratis and unencumbered with expectations is still generally pernicious from a biopolitical point of view.

4.1 Paradoxes of Development

All First World countries, and some others, give 'development aid' to Third World countries. This could be mistaken for a kind of global biopolitics, an attempt to make people in the Third World healthy, to extend their lives. I do not deny that aid does help people live. It is biological. It is also political, but it is no biopolitics. Biopolitics implies a relationship of state to population. Here there is no population constituted, nor does the state relate to it in the same way it would to its own population.

All the standard allegations against aid are true: aid budgets fall short of the official targets, which in themselves are insufficient, the money is wasted, spent at home on inefficient bureaucracies, etc. But even to the extent that it does reach its supposedly optimal destination, it is largely a catastrophe. This is not for a lack of good intentions. Clearly, the express intention of aid is to help the Third World and its people, to help countries to develop, and thereby to alleviate suffering. Of course, there are other motives too, but this does not negate its beneficent intention. However, there is no regular relationship between the intentions behind an action and its effects when it comes to such interventions, due to the complexity of the political, economic, and social interplays involved. I will argue that aid has generally had profoundly negative effects where 'development' is concerned. It thereby contributes unwittingly to the strategy of imperialism, including specifically biopolitical imperialism.

The biopolitical problem with aid concerns the relationship of the two poles required in the constitution of biopolitics, state and population. Development aid has always primarily taken the form of aid given by one government to another. This has not led to development, because there is no reason for recipient governments to use aid to create real development. Those in power rather first and foremost enrich themselves and their cronies, while pacifying populations, ensuring popular support sufficient to continue to rule, on the one hand, and satisfying donors to ensure the continuation of flows of aid on the other. Popular support can be procured by distributing aid as largesse—that is, not by building infrastructure, but by giving out free gifts, and indeed by spending money on repressive apparatuses with which to suppress discontent (and of course rather a lot of aid takes the form of military assistance eminently usable for this purpose).

Where donor satisfaction is concerned, while some evidence of progress may be required, the basic condition of aid is, on the contrary, the lack of development. That is, developing the country successfully would end the flow of aid. While development ought itself to provide an alternative source of income to government coffers, namely tax receipts, shifting to such a domestic source of funding for government raises difficult problems of accountability to taxpayers, that is to the population, who have a greater direct interest in and awareness of the progress of development. Thus aid to governments incentivises failure, making governments dependent on aid, rather than on their own people. Where even the most brutal regime in a hermetic state must be concerned with maintaining some kind of consent of the governed, even if by coercion and fear, and in cultivating the population as the source of the regime's power, to the extent that a government gets its money from foreign donors, it can simply ignore its populace, needing only to pacify them to the extent that they will not overthrow the regime.

That said, crony governments are often incompetent at using aid effectively to head off rebellion—indeed, it is biopolitics that is precisely the best means of doing this, as we have said. Moreover, the very concentration of funds in government hands tends actively to provoke rebellion. Aid-dependent governments, for example, distribute aid primarily to certain ethnic groups, causing others to be resentful. Government itself becomes the all-important prize to be captured in an aid-dependent economy, hence rebellion, coups, and civil war are likely outcomes.

Without aid dependence, or at least without dependence on peculiar external revenue sources more generally, the wealth of the government flows largely from the governed, and hence government is not a cash cow. In the biopolitical situation, as opposed to dependency, violent contestation can also occur, but around the use and abuse of biopolitics, with people demanding biopolitics be used or not used in certain ways. If rebels try to capture government in this situation, it is to capture a biopolitical apparatus to use it differently. The difference between recent guerrilla movements in Africa and Latin America can be schematically characterised as representing this difference between groups fighting simply to gain a slice of a pie and groups fighting to reorder society respectively. Though Latin American economies certainly suffer various kinds of dependency, they are less aid-dependent and more biopolitical than African ones. One could equally say the same thing of the difference between recent and colonial-era rebel movements in Africa. Anti-colonial rebels fought for control of the biopolitical apparatus of the colonial state—we saw this in South Africa, Zimbabwe, Namibia, Angola, Mozambique, and Algeria, countries where the biopolitical apparatuses put in place by settler-colonial regimes were substantial. In much of the continent, however, the post-colonial period has been punctuated by wars for the control of meagre state apparatuses, which nevertheless control substantial revenue flows from aid and license fees for resource exploitation from foreign conglomerates. Of course, most real situations are a mixture of both these types. Doubtless all countries today have some biopolitics, and most in the Third World exhibit some degree of aid dependency.

Now, the failure of giving aid to governments has in recent years been increasingly appreciated. This failure is generally conceptualised in terms of 'corruption' and 'bad governance'. That is, the cause is generally taken to be cultural, a matter (though not in so many words) of the primitive cultures of the Third World. In this way the Third World is blamed for its failure to develop despite the white man's copious philanthropic assistance. This way of thinking relates to the shift to neo-racism already covered in earlier chapters. Where once other peoples were thought of as racially incapable of equal advancement, we today know that people from the Third World are capable of equalling our achievements when removed from the context of their own countries. This implies that it is not even the 'culture' per se of the Third World, such as religion, that is to blame for underdevelopment, since successful immigrants may retain this culture. Rather, it is concluded that there is a specifically political culture that is bad in Third World countries. Hence hand-wringing concern about the ability of immigrants to absorb 'democratic values', accompanied by a general confidence that they will do so, which indeed indicates that the problem is endemic to polities not individuals.

The practical effect of these assumptions is the redirection of some aid from governments directly to the people: the state is cut out, as NGOs go directly into countries to minister aid themselves. This fails for much the same reason that the aid to governments did, albeit from the opposite direction: the people, rather than the government, now become dependent on aid. The people have less reason to care about the official politics of their country, to be involved in the political system, to try to change the government, or to support it, to pay taxes, etc. This in turn makes governments themselves even more reliant on aid: the situation tends towards one in which government and people exist in parallel, each beholden to the First World, with little connection between one another. The interdependency of government, people and economy is necessary to biopolitics. Aid encourages a mutual dependence of each of these agencies on aid rather than on each other.

It is argued that aid works a lot better when good govern-mental policies are in place.[41] Indeed it does, but this doesn't tell us how to produce the good governance to begin with. Craig Burnside and David Dollar suggest that we should withhold aid where good policy is not found. They perhaps think this will incentivise the development of good policy, as they understand it. I think it imperative, by contrast, simply because aid in the absence of good governance is likely actively to inhibit devel-opment. A number of eminent African economists—George Ayittey, James Shikwati, Yash Tandon—recognise this essential fact and share my conclusion that development aid should be stopped in order to foster development. They do not, however, recognise the extent to which what is needed is an endogenous development of biopolitics as a reciprocal relationship of state and population, by which the state tries to increase its power and the population fights back, establishing biopolitics as a compromise; they tend rather towards the liberal fantasy that it is civil society that does everything including producing the state.

This ignorance of the importance of the state as an institution, in favour of a focus on cultures of governance, is shared by the aid industry. Aid aims to foster the health of people in Third World nations on a sustainable and non-aid-dependent basis, but it cannot. Rather, in practice it works only to improve key health indicators, without biopolitics, at the cost of dependency.

Like so many aspects of biopolitical imperialism, aid dependence is due more to indifference than malevolence. Aid donors have little to no incentive to produce real development in Third World countries. The stakes for them are not biopolitical, but neo-colonial: they have geopolitical and commercial objectives in giving aid. The most extreme example of aid's indifference is perhaps the International Monetary Fund's structural adjustment policies, which amounted to a deliberate destruction of biopolitics in the periphery. While those responsible may have genuinely believed that they were helping, at least in the long term, such measures would never have been tolerated in a First World context, and this precisely because there decision-makers would be held more accountable for the negative consequences, because the decision-makers are themselves in the First World and because people in the First World have much more capacity to object effectively to things being done to them.

The sheer unthinking nature of biopolitical imperialism can be seen in the use of a fake inoculation programme by the US, in the effort to locate Osama bin Laden. In the context of a global battle against polio that was almost decisively won, where the only countries where it remained to be annihilated were Pakistan, Afghanistan and Nigeria, areas already justifiably suspicious of the intentions of Western interventions, the use of inoculation as a cover critically discredited the practice. In the years after bin Laden's assassination by US forces, polio has begun to spread again, constituting an international health emergency. There is no telling how many may die as a result—but they will not be likely to be in the First World, which can easily afford simply to continue to vaccinate its children.

The relatively small NGO aid sector is more genuine in its intention to help, of course, but in the end they too have no real stake in the outcome, only in convincing themselves and their donors that they are making a difference. The distance between donors and recipients is crucial here to maintaining these illusions.

Take, for example, the proverbial doctors without borders who flock to the Third World to treat people there. Such personnel generally visit briefly during time out from their First World careers, and rarely settle in Third World countries, and hence do little to build up a local biopolitics, but rather serve to reduce the impetus for a local biopolitics to be created endogenously. Of course, even if these doctors were to stay, they would constitute little more than biopolitical spit-back when viewed vis-à-vis the great theft of medical personnel, who leave the Third World for the First every day, never to move back.

NGOs pose as pedagogical agents, as teaching people to fish rather than merely giving them fish. But people in the Third World know how to fish. Of course, there are forms of knowledge that are lacking in the Third World, but this is not the major barrier to development. Nor is it even a lack of infrastructure that forms the main impediment, though this is perhaps a more significant barrier. It is not fundamentally a question of knowledge or ignorance, nor indeed of having or not having something, but of power structures.

4.2 Fostering Biopolitics

Is it completely impossible for aid to foster biopolitics? The sheer complexity of the social relations interacting with aid to produce or retard development make any absolute claims unreliable. I will spend the rest of this chapter considering two cases: firstly, the Marshall Plan, wherein development aid was apparently successful, asking what the difference was between this and the aid I have been criticising; secondly, cases of Third World countries which have actually developed, asking how these relate to aid.

The 1947–51 Marshall Plan by which America gave reconstruction aid to Europe in the aftermath of World War Two was the greatest aid programme in history. While some have cast doubt on the extent to which the Plan actually boosted European economic growth, it at least does not seem to have retarded it. It thus seems to stand as a counterexample to my claims about the biopolitical corrosiveness of aid.

There are several relevant differences between the Marshall Plan and contemporary aid to the Third World, however. One is that the former was a one-off exercise, limited in duration to only a few years, unlike the slow, never-ending drip of aid that the Third World has today. Ruling elites could thus not depend on it, because it was going to stop. My critique of aid thus does not apply to extraordinary aid in situations of acute emergency, for example, in response to wars or natural disasters, where it is a temporary stop-gap.

Another difference between the Marshall Plan and conventional development aid is that functioning biopolitics was entrenched in Europe, even if in some cases states and physical infrastructure had been temporarily shattered. Perhaps more decisive than this, moreover, was the strong motivation by all participants to produce a particular outcome: the Marshall Plan donor and recipients all desperately desired an economic recovery in Europe, because of a shared fear of the expansion of communism, which had just overrun Eastern Europe. This meant giving the workers of Western Europe enough to lure them away from communism, while building up militarised economies capable of resisting Soviet armies (it should be mentioned that initially the Plan was to include the Soviet Union—this would have been an attempt to include and placate the Soviets, a scarcely less urgent desire; as it was, the Cold War erupted in the midst of negotiations, changing the complexion of the Plan at a crucial moment). The Marshall Plan was a struggle for survival by capitalism. No such immediate, self-interested urgency underlies aid donations today; rather, as I have noted, they are marked by indifference towards development outcomes.

Another difference is that the Marshall Plan was not merely a close collaboration between governments. Rather, it included a variety of stakeholders within the various *nations*. There was a recognition in particular that the working class and trades unions had to be involved, as well as the private sector. The project was thus deliberately biopolitical, feeding into a major expansion of biopolitics in recipient countries during the period.

We can compare this unfavourably to the later effort of the European Union to build up the economies of Greece and Ireland by pouring money into them. This seemed successful for a time. We could have said that since the EU was bringing these countries inside it, there would be no problem. But the EU is not really a state, let alone a biopolitical state. It could not administer this aid, but rather gave it to governments. In Greece, it was used to prop up an expanding bureaucracy without an organic connection to the population through tax income. That is, the Greek economy was pumped full of cash, without any basis of sustainability, producing dependency.

One might ask in relation to this how the Third World got what biopolitics it has in the first place. The answer, in short, is that it was installed largely during colonialism, a phase in which Western governments as more or less direct rulers actually fostered biopolitics. Colonialism of course was not intended as a biopolitical enterprise, and indeed initially destroyed much that was proto-biopolitical in colonised lands, but colonisers would later adopt biopolitical methods, tried and tested in the metropole, to control subjugated populations, though thanatopolitics retained a larger role in the colonies than in the metropoles. The establishment of biopolitics in the colonies thus followed a broadly similar pattern to what had occurred earlier in the metropoles: governors' concerns are initially confined to the well-being of the elite, and hence with epidemic diseases, but expand under the influence of popular demands for greater welfare to cover the population. In India, for example, biopolitics was introduced first to care for the British occupiers, then their Indian personnel, then the whole population—though of course, there was always a hierarchy of concern maintained between these categories. The British established a commercial domination in India, which became a political domination, which led them to become interested in biopolitics as a way of managing the populace politically and economically.[42] The establishment of biopolitics was closely related to the inclusion of Indians in positions of authority within British India. It can be understood partially as a series of concessions by Britain to Indian resistance, aimed at preventing what was nevertheless the eventual outcome, Indian independence.

Such is the general pattern of (post)colonial biopolitics, though of course each country has its peculiarities. The remainder of the world that was neither Europe nor colonised by Europe had to develop biopolitics endogenously. In such states— China, Turkey, Iran—biopolitics was deliberately brought about in modernisation programmes by Western-influenced parties, in a context of intense civil struggles.

All these cases are unlike aid, where the donor is not in a state-like relationship with the population. This is not to say I advocate a restoration of colonialism: the abolition of colonialism is a necessary step towards the abolition of imperialism, just not a sufficient one. Colonialism itself can be presumed to operate as a brake to biopolitical development—the fact that colonial authorities instituted biopolitical measures does not imply that there would otherwise not be biopolitics—but its absence is certainly not an automatic advantage in this regard.

4.3 Development Despite Development

And yet, it seems the contemporary Third World is at last developing. The media talk insistently about the 'rise of the African/Indian/Chinese middle class'.

Now, this can mislead. 'Middle class' is here defined as people with any disposable income. Still, there has been undeniable economic growth in much of the (former) Third World. Of course, economic development does not necessarily equate to biopolitical development. Today, the hegemony of neoliberalism, of the idea that the state should be small and noninterventionist and that almost everything should be left to the market, means that governments are not that interested in biopolitics. That said, there are few Third World countries that have not recorded at least modest growth in their Human Development Index score in recent years. Then again, biopolitics cannot be reduced to this, partly because some of its indicators are educational and economic rather than biological, but more importantly because biopolitics is about the government of the population and is not reducible to statistics.

In some Third World countries biopolitics has definitely developed, however. Yet this does not disprove my theses, since I hold only that imperialism retards development, not that it definitively stymies it.

The most dramatic developmental story of recent times is of course China. Its growth has primarily been economic and has certainly been unequal, but its government has begun to extend biopolitical care for its population markedly: it has deliberately used the nation's newfound prosperity to introduce a range of social welfare measures: unemployment insurance, maternity benefits, pension funds, and universal healthcare.[43]

China avoided the inimical effects of biopolitical imperialism outlined earlier in this chapter. It spent decades largely cut off from the capitalist world economy, establishing control of the state over its population and economy, guided by Maoist ideology to 'serve the people'. When after Mao's death China's leaders definitively adopted a 'capitalist road' of development in the late 1970s, they did so with a strong state and rudimentary biopolitics already established. China received comparatively little foreign aid: after China's economy opened up, aid did flow in, in the low billions of dollars, but this was unimportant relative to the size of China's economy even then, merely a few dollars per person. China in effect owes the robustness of its development to anti-imperialist policies and a sheer size that prevented the depredations of imperialism from stymying it.

One might question this claim of mine on the basis that the much smaller and pro-imperialist Asian Tiger countries (South Korea, Taiwan, Singapore, and Hong Kong) achieved something similar in terms of growth in the 1990s to what China has a decade later. However, these economies resembled China's in not receiving significant amounts of development aid, and—except for South Korea—in not taking on sizable loans, and having very strong states with substantial biopolitics in the areas of housing and healthcare. In this their case resembles the Western European reconstruction of several decades before: imperialism fostered their development precisely as a bulwark against China, rather than allowing them to become aid dependencies.

It should be noted, however, that China's biopolitical development has been marked by a bifurcation of its population into rural and urban components that at least approaches biopolitical imperialism within its own borders. China in effect has internal borders to the movement of people in the form of the *hukou* system, which restricts citizens to living in certain areas. The Chinese boom has been largely premised on hundreds of millions of poor workers from rural areas moving to cities where they are paid very low wages, work long hours, and live in pitiful conditions. They are generally not officially allowed to settle in the cities, but remain classified as rural residents. Many are not even legally allowed to work in the cities where they do, but are effectively a form of internal illegal immigrant. However, the residency conditions are not enforced rigorously—people are no longer 'repatriated' to the area of their official residency. They are only prevented from accessing a range of services outside of that area, including health services in the cities where they now live, again resembling the condition of many immigrants in the West Although China has in the past decade shifted from a majority agrarian to a majority urban society, it has done so only on this basis.

This pattern of exclusion has been sustained through one of the most extraordinary biopolitical measures of our age, the 'one-child policy'. This policy dates to 1977, an artefact of Deng's capitalist road (Mao, by contrast, deliberately fostered population growth). The policy is aimed officially at curtailing demographic increase in China as an economic necessity. However, it applies primarily to urban areas. Ethnic minorities, mostly rural, are partially or totally exempt. Han Chinese in the countryside can officially have two children if their first child is a girl, and in practice have as many children as they like. This means that there is a constant supply of cheap labour from the countryside to serve the cities, compensating for the fact that the city population is not endogenously replacing itself. Because rural migrants to cities cannot access urban schools, they are compelled to send their children back to grow up in the countryside, ensuring that the pattern of rural-urban migration will continue into the next generation.

Given the extent of the difference in biopolitical services

applied in different regions, the parasitism of urban on rural China could be described as biopolitical imperialism, and indeed as biopolitical colonialism since rural China is not politically independent of urban China. It should be noted that reform of the *hukou* system in the direction of universal healthcare has been officially announced, but at present it remains unclear to what extent this will be realised.

So, China's economic rise is premised on cheap labour, on poverty, on terrible conditions for its proletariat. Chinese cities lie shrouded in toxic smog and workers remove mercury from broken computers with their bare hands. It is premised also on the wealth of the West that buys its produce. Since the Global Financial Crisis (GFC), it is commonly inveighed that China must reorient its economy to domestic consumption. Indeed this is so. This of course sets up the old impasse of trying to sell to one's own workforce: where does the profit come from? China's logical move is to expand its sales to the Third World, to Africa in particular. Such searches for new markets are as old as capitalism itself.

China has begun over the last decade to intervene decisively in African economies, building infrastructure, which has been a major driver of Africa's own newfound economic development. The scale of China's investment in Africa can be overstated, however: it is only a small portion of China's overall OFDI and it has also declined significantly from a sudden and vertiginous spike in 2008, immediately before the GFC. The scale of Chinese investment varies moreover from country to country. It tends to be proportional to the size of countries' economies: the continent's largest economy, Nigeria, receives the greatest Chinese investment, though there are also anomalies: Egypt, the third biggest economy on the continent, is a relatively minor recipient compared to middle-sized economies like Chad, Tanzania, and Zambia.

The extent to which Chinese involvement in Africa is a new

imperialism or even a new colonialism is as yet an open question, but it seems to be much less harmful than Western interventions on the continent, and seems be a stimulus to African development in a way that Western involvement is not. This is not to say that China is less self-interested than the West, just that its modus operandi is different and less toxic. China is sometimes cited as having given enormous amounts of 'aid' to Africa, but this is mostly a matter of long-term, favourable loans, specifically to finance development projects, which are in turn mostly run by Chinese companies, meaning that effectively the Chinese are doing the work of building African infrastructure—this resembles the Marshall Plan at least as much as it does Western development loans. This aid does not have corrupting effects. China trades its consumer products to Africa for primary produce almost dollar-for-dollar. Because there is no major wage disparity, the problem of unequal exchange is negligible. Where Western companies bring in highly paid managers from the West and use African labour, the Chinese supply their own workforce. This denies much needed job opportunities to Africans, and hinders the development of local capacity, but it means the overall balance of flows of people between China and Africa are completely the opposite of those between Africa and the West. China sends large numbers of doctors to work on the continent, without stealing any. There is African migration to China, but many more Chinese move to Africa than Africans to China. These Chinese are long-term migrants, but they are not settler colonists. Doubtless they earn more than the average African, but they are generally workers and small businesspeople, not ranchers and factory owners. There are resentments against Chinese migrants from Africans, and the pattern of Chinese trade with Africa, exporting manufactured goods and importing raw materials, recapitulates to an extent the old imperial economic relationship,[44] but if China is engaging in imperialism in Africa, it is a minor one relative to the entrenched imperialism of the Western powers.

China also has no history of or capacity to intervene militarily in Africa (though it has this decade for the first time ever sent troops to participate in UN peacekeeping on the continent), whereas the American and French militaries in particular continue regularly to intervene directly in Africa; the US military has an Africa-specific command structure, Africom, and US forces train in and with the forces of most African nations. China by contrast avows not to interfere in the internal affairs of other countries and not to engage in acts of aggression. While it is wise to be suspicious of the veracity of such claims, it is worth noting that America in particular does not even make them, and that it arrogates a right to global interference in almost everything.

Far from being an imperialist power, China remains, in effect, a victim of imperialism (particularly in the form of unequal exchange). In pure economic terms, the Chinese population is doing a lot of work effectively on credit, despite the cut-price rates at which they do it, being paid only with US securities given the massive balance of trade deficits in its trade with the First World. Moreover, much of the profit accruing from China to the West ends up back in the West: 64 per cent of wealthy Chinese are either in the process of emigrating to the West or planning to do so, and are moving large amounts of money offshore.[45]

The political importance of Chinese exports to the First World should not be underestimated: clothes and other consumer goods have become cheap in the West as a result of China's industriali-sation and that of other major Asian countries. This affects Western biopolitics: cheap imports change the costs associated with welfare and healthcare in the West, since welfare recipients buy cheap Chinese-made necessities, and much that is used in Western hospitals, for example, day-to-day, is also of Third World manufacture (although it's hard to estimate the extent of this; while the NHS has a transparent supply chain, its suppliers themselves do not). Chinese workers die in mines and commit suicide under the conditions that generate cost savings for UK hospitals.

An amelioration of such Third World workers' conditions is often proposed in terms of 'ethical' consumerism, by which First World consumers are enjoined not to buy things made by people who are overly exploited. One problem with this discourse is that it defines 'fair trade' in a way that ignores unequal exchange, including unequal biopolitics: workers in Third World countries do not have the same access to healthcare and welfare as Western workers, and the absence of this access is embodied in the lower prices of Third World goods. That is, the cheapness of Third World goods is premised not only on lower wages, but lower life expectancy, higher infant mortality, etc. The great excuse here is that trade will enrich the Third World. Indeed, a boycott of Third World products would be of no help. It is not the case, however, that buying them is an act of beneficence, even in the case of the 'win-win' situation suggested by the smiling faces that accompany the sales pitch of Fair Trade sellers.

The rationale of ethical consumerism is the same as Western dealings with the Third World in general, namely that development will proceed automatically through the magic of the Invisible Hand. It is simply false that wages and biopolitical conditions automatically rise, however. They rise only where there is action to make this happen. In China, for example, the spectre of mass dissent, protests and wildcat strikes are pressuring the government to raise living standards to some extent. While the Chinese state is not a workers' state by any definition, it is capable of raising living standards to ensure social cohesion.

The Indian state, by contrast, does not appear to be willing or able to do this. India long resisted imperialism after gaining its independence, partially closing itself off from foreign direct investment, but the essential problem of entrenched class and caste power in the country remained and inhibited the development of a mass biopolitics beyond a certain point. India has free healthcare, importantly, but most Indians remain endemically poor. India's economic growth in recent years has been massive, but smaller than China's, concentrated in an even smaller minority than China's is. I must acknowledge, however, at the time of writing, the extraordinary and clearly biopolitical drive by the new administration of Narendra Modi in 2014 to build millions of toilets—though of course in itself hardly enough to address systemic problems.

We may also compare the pattern of India's growth to date unfavourably to Brazil's. After decades of right-wing governments, the left took power in Brazil in 2002, since when the economy has grown strongly, albeit with a significant shock during 2009 due to the GFC, before quickly rebounding to even greater growth. Biological indicators have improved slowly but steadily over these years due to the left-wing government's reforms, the centrepiece of which was the Fome Zero programme. This was wide-ranging, and thoroughly biopolitical, taking in nutrition, vaccination, and financial aid to ensure adequate nutrition and education for all citizens. It cut child poverty and improved school attendance. It has been attacked from the left for propping up capitalism by ending some of its more extreme injustices without changing things at a systemic level, but this can be rightly said of any biopolitical development within capitalism.

The general lesson here is that economic development creates opportunities for biopolitical development, but the former does not automatically produce the latter. It is also possible to biopoliticise without economic growth. This is shown by the case of Cuba, a great exception, which has for decades had biopolitical indicators and a healthcare system on a par with the First World, while its economy has remained resolutely Third World, and indeed at times suffered serious decline.

Biopolitical development can occur where the state and/or

population is determined to bring it about. Aid inhibits each of these from developing such a determination, and thereby inhibits the development of biopolitics.

4.4 Domestic Dependency?

Could this critique apply not only to aid, but to charitable NGOs operating within the countries from which they draw their support? That is to say, if aid inhibits the development of biopolitics by preventing the formation of appropriate biopolitical relations between state and population, might not charity not controlled by the state also have a similar effect within societies?

Domestic philanthropy did indeed inhibit the development of biopolitics, I would suggest, but only up to the point where it became part of biopolitics. The creation of biopolitics entailed a struggle between the state and the Church over the care of people's lives, the former wresting control from the latter. This was a struggle that was violent and bloody, if complicatedly interrelated with other struggles in early modern Europe. NGO activity in Western countries is today for the most part subordinated to the state. NGOs continually appeal to the state to implement measures and to fund them. Only in extraordinary situations within biopolitical societies do NGOs operate against the state. An example of this, though its risible marginality indicates how rare and unimportant such cases are, is the Church of Scientology. Unlike mainstream religions, which are content to work with the state in the service of temporal goals, Scientology will not. It is precisely for this reason that the German state banned it, though the fact that other states tolerate it indicates how marginal it is as a threat: it does not seek to usurp the state's biopolitical function, with the exception of the institution of medical psychiatry, which it both vociferously denounces and sets up its own alternative to. One can mention, however, a number of other fundamentalist religious organisations and extremist political groups that engage in biopolitical operations outside of the control of the state on a more ambitious scale: the Black Panthers, the Egyptian Muslim Brotherhood, the neo-Nazi Golden Dawn in Greece. All these movements specifically fed people in operations designed to circumvent the state's authority, and all have suffered prodigious state repression. It is of course not the distribution of food itself that drew the state's ire— otherwise the state would repress Hare Krishnas—but their attempt to set themselves up as an alternative to the state. That the US repressed the Black Panthers but not Scientology is indicative of the extent to which the former and not the latter was trying to establish an alternative state.

Within the contemporary biopolitical welfare state, the much-maligned 'welfare dependency' of a layer of the population is nevertheless akin to aid dependency, not because of the operation of non-state actors, but in relation to the state and population themselves. As with aid dependency, while the right object to it on grounds of a morality of self-reliance, from a biopolitical perspective the problem is that the state has no reason to care about this layer insofar as they do not contribute to it, only an interest in controlling them, which then indeed opens the way for the political right to remove their welfare. Indeed, welfare dependency is indicative of a welfare state that his shifted from providing a safety net towards being a form of social pacification, though doubtless it always had both functions to varying extents.

There is another effect we may refer to tangentially here, which is not biopolitical imperialism so much as biopolitical colonisation, where communities are forcibly incorporated into a First World national biopolitics. I am thinking particularly again of the treatment of Australian Aborigines. Implementation of biopolitical measures has always been fragmentary in remoter communities, but where it is implemented it is toxic in much the same way aid dependency is. This is due to the fact that it bypasses the formerly sovereign political structures of indigenous communities and renders them irrelevant. One might also refer to the treatment of Roma people in Europe, for example. The incorporation of such communities into a metropolitan population fails resolutely to create the biopolitical outcomes that are assumed to follow automatically from the standard measures, because this form of biopolitical care severs existing bonds of community reliance. Over time peoples forced into populations in this way may develop relationships with the state, but these cannot be presumed to form automatically, and during a long interim period, alienation is thoroughgoing and the results fatal in many cases, such that the survival of the community is threatened.

5

War

The aggressiveness of liberal imperialism is not that of Nazi Germany, though the distinction may seem academic to a Vietnamese peasant who is being gassed or incinerated. – Noam Chomsky

5.1 Vietnam, Iraq, Afghanistan

According to Foucault, biopolitics has a perverse relationship to war. While biopolitics accentuates life and banishes death, it has actually produced the bloodiest wars in human history, the world wars of the twentieth century and their attendant genocides. The preoccupation with preserving life justifies its opposite. This justification occurs in two directions, on Foucault's account. On the one hand, the way in which the enemy is presented in biopolitical societies, dehumanised by racism and imagined as a biological threat to the population, makes it not only possible but desirable to neutralise them, justifying their extermination. On the other hand, since external enemies are viewed as threats to the existence of the population itself, the population can countenance its own exposure to risk of death up to and including its complete extinction to combat these threats. Together, the biologistic vilification of the other and the risking of the population produce a new phenomenon, what has been called 'total war', a war not just between sovereigns or states or armies, but between entire populations.

Imperialism is forged and enforced by war. Imperialist police actions, wars by the First World on the Third, have always been on a more modest scale than those between imperialist nations—which of course owes mainly to the dissymmetry in power between the two sides in such cases. Though some Third World states possess nuclear weapons, for example, the West to date has only prosecuted war against Third World nations that pose no serious existential threat to it, but rather only threaten their economic and political interests. The risk this licenses on the part of Western populations is limited. Indeed, during a brief period in the 1990s it seemed that the First World had ceased to countenance serious risk in its confrontations with its outside, ushering in an era of 'zero death war' in which its combat casualties were minimised (although not literally reduced to zero, since no human activity is entirely without risk of death). This doctrine, however, only meant minimisation of risk *on our side*. Third World enemies continued to be slaughtered en masse.

The extent of avoidance of deaths on our side was made possible by making war increasingly distant: in the 1990s, wars were conducted primarily by air, with bombers flying out of range of enemy defences. This did not imply fewer deaths on the enemy side, however: to fight a war in this way is blunt and partially blind, failing to discriminate between civilians and soldiers, or between resisting and surrendering troops, white flags and entreaties for mercy unseen and unheard. This phenomenon has in this century gone even further as drones have replaced bombers , all risk to the pilot negated. Drone warfare ameliorates the problem of war in the age of biopolitics that the soldier must embody in one subjectivity both biopolitics and thanatopolitics. The soldier is, like any Western subject, required today to be peaceable in his dealings with most people, within his own society, to protect and promote life, yet in certain specific circumstances is supposed to kill and maim people. This division is fraught, and soldiers overstep the bounds of allowed killing in combat and civilian life: some soldiers and veterans harm others within their own society, though the ones they are most likely to harm are themselves. The health of the subject is threatened by the mission to kill, the health of society is threatened by the killers in its midst. Doubtless something like post-traumatic stress disorder has always existed, but it is certainly only in this conjunction of biopolitics and thanatopolitics that PTSD is named as such as a medical disorder. The population will thus benefit from not having its members experience the viscerality of war: such an experience is minimised if not eliminated in drone warfare.

Still, this century, during the 'War on Terror' waged since 2001, risks have been countenanced that were not during the preceding two decades. Fewer than 400 American servicepersons died in all the wars of the 1990s, and a similar number during the 80s, compared with over 6,000 US war dead during the 00s, although this is still not much more than 10 per cent as many as America lost in the Vietnam War during the 1960s and early 1970s. I would contend that America countenanced a much higher scale of death in the Cold War conflicts in Korea and Vietnam because international communism was seen as an existential threat to the US population: communism threatened to take over the whole world, and the Soviet Union's nuclear programme threatened genuine annihilation. Nevertheless, the eventual turning of US public opinion against the Vietnam War would indicate precisely that the existential threat was not perceived as acute enough to justify the US death toll that accumulated. The vastly greater Vietnamese death toll in the war, by contrast, was not a major concern of most of the US public.

This century's renewed death tolerance relative to the 80s and 90s is the consequence of a perception of renewed threat to the US population. This perception was occasioned by the attacks of the 11th September 2001 ('September 11' or '9-11'), which killed almost 3,000 people. This was the largest loss of US civilian life in a single attack in the country's history. America is less used to having its cities attacked than many other First World countries. Its reaction was predictably hyperbolic. I say it was 'hyperbolic', because the attack caused very little damage to the US demographically or economically, and because a recurrence of the event was highly unlikely: the 9-11 attacks were possible only because the standard response of aeroplane passengers and crew to hijacking attempts was to yield control to the hijackers and wait for release, whereas these attacks made such compliance by passengers and crew unlikely in future. It was effectively a one-off exploitation of a loophole. The reaction was nonetheless predictable, that Americans would not tolerate foreigners deliberately killing so many members of its population. Never mind that ten times as many Americans were killed in the same year by Americans using firearms;[46] this is a regular internal feature of the American situation, not a terrifyingly unexpected external threat.

America's response has encompassed two major wars, its invasions of Afghanistan and Iraq. The former occurred almost immediately after the 11th September attacks, aimed apparently at capturing a single individual alleged to be responsible for the attacks, but having the broader aim of pacifying a country which was seen as a breeding ground for terrorism. The US demanded the Taliban, the de facto government of most of Afghanistan, hand over America's prime suspect, Osama bin Laden, and when the Taliban failed to comply immediately, the US invaded and deposed them, killing thousands of Afghans.

The legal justification for this action was that it was a response to an act of war against the US, thus self-defence. But the relationship of Afghanistan to the attacks was tangential. The Afghan state, such as it was (that is, the Taliban), had done nothing more than harbour someone who had allegedly funded the attacks, and not during the period of time when he had allegedly done so (he had at that time been in Sudan). No hijacker was Afghan, although some—but not most—of them had spent time there.

Bin Laden was eventually assassinated by US forces in Pakistan, a decade later. This demonstrated two things. Firstly, it indicated the type of operation required to kill a single individual: not the invasion and occupation of a whole country, but a targeted attack by special forces. Secondly, it demonstrated that the interest in bin Laden was not to try him, not to find the person responsible for 9-11, but to kill him, that is, to neutralise a perceived threat.

Nevertheless, the possibility that further deaths of US citizens might emanate from the territory of Afghanistan was seen as giving the US the right to occupy that entire country and kill people who might resist this occupation, even before they had displayed any actual resistance. This in effect defined self-defence so broadly it could justify any military action whatsoever. The expansive logic of 'pre-emptive' defence was seen more clearly in America's invasion of Iraq soon after. Michael Dillon and Julian Reid have suggested that 'pre-emptive war is a natural corollary of the biopoliticization of... war'.[47] But strictly speaking pre-emptive war is time-honoured: it has always made strategic sense to neutralise any potential threat as early as possible. What is new is simply the biopolitical complexion given to this, that it is necessary to wage pre-emptive war to neutralise threats not only to one's power or interests, but to the population as such. It then includes not only pre-emptive war against states that might attack your state, but in order to control sub-state actors to prevent them attacking your citizens. This logic ultimately licences the total control of the globe down to the level of every individual, and this has become the asymptotic *telos* of American policy.

The logic of threat neutralisation became more blatant in the 2003 invasion of Iraq, a country that had no demonstrable link to 9-11 or any other recent act of terrorism against the US, despite the fact that the US population largely inferred from the fact their government was invading Iraq that there was such a link. The invasion of Iraq was the next order of business in a bid for greater control of the geopolitical situation, pre-empting possible future threats. This does link it to 9-11 inasmuch as 9-11 produced a general drive to increase US 'homeland security', and inasmuch as it led to a popular bellicosity in America. While the US government circumspectly avoided falsely alleging that Iraq was responsible for 9-11, allowing the population to reach this conclusion on their own, it did perpetrate a big lie as public pretext for the action, namely that Iraq had 'weapons of mass destruction' ('WMDs'). There was no positive evidence of this (and even if it were true, it would have posed no direct threat to any of the countries that invaded), but the US and UK demanded that Saddam Hussein prove that he did not have them. That is, they demanded that he prove a negative, which is impossible. The only way indeed that the West could prove there were no weapons of mass destruction in Iraq was to take control of Iraq's entire territory, which they did, discovering that indeed the weapons did not exist.

Though the war was legitimised with the US public through misinformation, there was a certain public trust in the government to act in America's security interests which was not entirely misplaced, inasmuch as the public too wanted a world made totally safe, hence wanted their government to control the globe.

The 2003 invasion was only the latest act in a more or less continuous campaign against Iraq by America and its allies since 1991. Indeed, it is still not entirely clear that this war has conclusively ended. This long war has smashed the nation of Iraq, killing perhaps a million of its inhabitants, perhaps significantly more. These two decades of war are commonly conceptualised as a series of distinct actions: the war over Kuwait in 1991, the subsequent sanctions, the invasion of 2003, the occupation after that. A clear commonality of all its phases, however, is the leading role taken by the US.

This war began in response to Saddam Hussein's 1990 invasion of Kuwait. Hussein's annexation of a sovereign country was a violation of international norms, and at this extraordinary moment after the thawing of the Cold War, the Soviet Union, then on the verge of collapse, backed America against Iraq, producing a substantial, though not unanimous, international consensus for military action, which was duly authorised by the United Nations Security Council.

The consequent war was conducted and commanded principally by the US military, although it involved a diverse multinational coalition. It went far beyond merely enforcing the UN resolution by extirpating Iraqi forces from Kuwait. It began with an enormous and prolonged aerial bombardment not of Iraqi forces in Kuwait, but of Iraq itself. The aim was, prior to any ground war with Iraqi forces, to destroy Iraq's capacity to wage war by destroying its infrastructure. We were told at the time via press briefings replete with grainy black and white video from American planes that 'smart bombs' had made civilian casualties a thing of the past. When such a bomb destroyed a Baghdad air raid shelter killing more than 400 civilians, the Western news media on the ground reacted with scepticism and suggested that the Iraqis had staged the whole thing. In reality allied bombing was, if not entirely indiscriminate, very broadly targeted and designed to devastate the country and terrorise its people—the same tactic that would be dubbed 'shock and awe' during the 2003 invasion. While officially the distinction between combatants and non-combatant civilians in modern war is held sacrosanct, since in a biopolitical nation the population as a whole produces and supports the capacity for war, this distinction is less tenable in modernity than ever before from a military point of view and is always elided in practice.

We must admit of course that imperialist warmongers do show some concern with the lives of people in the Third World during their operations, just very little. One may note, for example, the case of the dropping of food alongside cluster bombs during the US invasion of Afghanistan, with both packaged in yellow such that they were not always distinguishable from one another.[48] Here, we see a globally recognised biopolitical imperative—that no one should be allowed simply to starve to death—come into absurd conflict with the principle that 'collateral damage' in a just war is acceptable. We see this too in occupied Palestine, where Israel meticulously allows enough nutrition through to prevent Palestinians starving to death,[49] but then slaughters them in their thousands in efforts to kill 'militants'. In such a situation, the food aid is biopolitical backwash relative to the scale of destruction unleashed.

One of the few places which has a clearly protected status in modern warfare is the hospital (even though one can of course easily construct an argument justifying attacks on hospitals on the basis that they heal wounded soldiers and send them back to battle). In Iraq, hospitals were one of the few forms of infrastructure not deliberately targeted. The targeting of infrastructure has biopolitical effects such that the avoidance of medical facilities seems hypocritical or arbitrary, however. Eric Rouleau noted that in the 1991 war, the allies used air strikes

to systematically destroy or cripple Iraqi infrastructure and industry: electric power stations (92 per cent of installed capacity destroyed), refineries (80 per cent of production capacity), petrochemical complexes, telecommunications centers (including 135 telephone networks), bridges (more than 100), roads, highways, railroads, hundreds of locomotives and boxcars full of goods, radio and television broadcasting stations, cement plants, and factories producing aluminum, textiles, electric cables, and medical supplies.[50]

The biopolitical corollaries of this destruction were dire. The loss of such basic infrastructure was devastating to the operation of medical facilities (hospitals lost power, ambulances could not move, medicines were in short supply) and nutrition (food could not be distributed, water could not be treated to make it potable, irrigation for agriculture was damaged so food yields collapsed). The bombing killed thousands of civilians directly,[51] but still more by its longer term effects. One 1991 Pentagon briefing showed a bridge over which a car had just passed blowing up, touted as another example of the clean and victimless air campaign. But many deaths were consequent on the infrastructural devastation of which this was a part. As Noam Chomsky puts it, the air war was 'a form of biological warfare, having little relation to driving Iraq from Kuwait—rather, designed for long-term US political ends'.[52]

Long-term rather than immediate aims were also reflected in the bombing of thousands of Iraqi troops and non-Iraqi civilians as they fled Kuwait. When allied ground troops finally moved into Kuwait, they met with almost no resistance, but retreating Iraqis were nonetheless massacred. Far from being about forcing them to leave Kuwait, the massacre effectively blocked the main road out of town.

One saw already in the 1991 campaign the dual policy that would characterise the behaviour of the US and her closest allies, in particular the UK, towards Iraq until the final invasion more than twelve years later. One objective was what came to be described as 'regime change', that is, deposing Saddam Hussein. This objective was explicitly enshrined in US law by the 1998 Iraq Liberation Act. The other was to degrade Iraq's capacity to wage war. This explicitly figured as the demand that Iraq give up what would come to be called 'weapons of mass destruction', which is to say, chemical, biological, and nuclear weapons, but was pursued more generally, through the destruction of Iraqi military and civilian infrastructure.

Iraq's defeat in the 1991 war led to revolts. These began on the 1st March, the day after the ceasefire with the allies had begun, against the Ba'ath regime in the Shi'ite South and Kurdish North of Iraq. They enjoyed initial great success, but were crushed for the most part by the end of March. In support of the rebellions, several of the allied countries, principally of course the US, declared a 'no-fly zone' in northern Iraq to prevent the Iraqi government bombing Kurds. A second no-fly zone was declared in the South the following year in support of internecine resistance there. These principally involved arrogating the right to shoot down any Iraqi government aircraft in the areas designated. Fictitious authorisation from the UN was claimed for these interventions, in a pattern of creative interpretation of international law that would continue in relation to Iraq in years to come.

These no fly-zones continued for over a decade, constituting the military component of the continuation of the allies' dual mission during this time. When Iraq attacked allied patrolling aircraft, the allies bombed Iraqi military facilities, killing hundreds.

While the air strikes played a role in preventing the Iraqi regime from regaining control over the entire country, they did not have a major biopolitical impact. The biopolitical damage during this period occurred through an instrument genuinely approved by the UN, sanctions to enforce a ban on Iraq possessing WMDs. These sanctions compounded the demographic effects of the infrastructural destruction wrought by the 1991 bombing, killing hundreds of thousands, primarily through an increase in child mortality. Although food and medical supplies were meant to be exempt from sanctions, in practice both were severely restricted. Sanctions of course follow an old thanatopolitical logic, that of the siege: they work by starving people. In the age of biopolitics, however, entire national populations are besieged. Thus, until 2003, imperialists pursued their aims primarily by targeting not the Iraqi state, but rather its population, again hoping to produce an uprising, with the explicit aim being Iraqi WMD disarmament.

The policy effectively achieved this aim, but the West continued to prosecute the aim of regime change, and continued to insist that Iraq had not disarmed, against all evidence to the contrary. Iraq was duly, finally invaded by ground forces in 2003, quickly toppling Hussein. When it was proven that Hussein had indeed disarmed himself years before, this ostensible justification for the invasion was quickly buried under rhetoric about the brutality of the Hussein regime towards its own citizens, ignoring the enormous scale of death the allies' own actions had wrought in the country, and the need to bring democracy to Iraq.

The invaders did indeed eventually install a system of government resembling the Western model of representative democracy. In the interim they generated a continuous resistance to the occupation, particularly by members of the previously dominant Sunni sect. The invasion and occupation resulted in the deaths of at least 100,000 Iraqi non-combatants.[53] They also destroyed more of the basic infrastructure of the country, not only physical infrastructure, but also the human infrastructure of the state, with the occupiers deliberately dismantling its bureaucracy and military in order to ensure that the previous regime could not reconstitute itself. In the ensuing power vacuum, Iraq spiralled into chaos and civil war. Millions fled Iraq, disproportionately technically skilled people, such as doctors.

In light of these results, the most common narrative about the 2003 invasion today is that it was an error; that the George W. Bush administration failed to understand the difficulties they would encounter. The American regime indeed seem to have believed blithely that removing Saddam Hussein from power would automatically lead to the emergence of democracy in Iraq. This reflects their deeply held liberalism, by which certain civic arrangements are seen as natural and automatic, and the state largely an artificial impost. The naïvety of this fantasy was quickly exposed: the removal of the state superstructure was a catastrophe, particularly in biopolitical terms. Such considerations seem simply not to have figured in the invaders' plans: they promised 'liberty' and even 'prosperity' for the natives, but never health.

Casting the invasion as a failure, however, seems to imply it was a kind of anomalous experiment. Yet on the contrary it followed a long-established pattern of imperialist war. Compare the previous war in which between 1941 and 1975 a changing cast of imperialist powers made war on Vietnam in attempts to control it, killing millions of people. It did terrible damage to Vietnam, damage which that country has barely recovered from even forty years later. This war too is often cast retrospectively as a strategic error. I would maintain it was not. If America could not prevent Vietnam becoming Communist, as it aimed to—by subsidising the French and the Vietnamese war efforts and ultimately by massive direct intervention—and failed to do, it could destroy Vietnam such that it could not pose so much of a threat to Western interests.

The 1991 war on Iraq was supposed to be of a fundamentally different type to the Vietnam War, a UN-sanctioned post-Cold War just war. In fact, the difference extended only to America having the ambitions of a quicker victory and lower casualties. Its modus operandi in Iraq was otherwise essentially similar, namely a lesser version of General Curtis LeMay's advice that the US bomb North Vietnam 'back into the Stone Age'. The American war on Vietnam had also principally been an air war, in which more than seven million tonnes of bombs were dropped, coming close to four times the total number of bombs dropped by all sides during the Second World War. The bombing of Iraq was on nothing like this scale, but nevertheless as Rouleau says (and as Tariq Aziz alleges was the explicit American intention) the Western allies managed to bomb 'Iraq back to the preindustrial age'. Rudimentary biopolitics did survive, but it has never recovered to anything like its pre-war level. In Afghanistan, by contrast, decade after decade of superpower invasions and superpower-sponsored warfare has left little to no functioning biopolitics. The 'medieval' nature of

Taliban-ruled Afghanistan, often imputed to either the Taliban's ideology or even to Islam itself, has at least as much to do with this wholesale degradation of the capacity of the country to govern itself in any more sophisticated way.

The West would optimally like the rest of the world to consist of functional states that served its interests. However, it is clearly a better outcome from its point of view to destroy states than have them be functional states hostile to its interests. We can go further and suggest that in fact functional states will by dint of their functionality not serve the West's interests, but their own interests, so in fact, though the West dreams of pliant functional states, its clients are always dysfunctional in practice. The logic of Western policy is in effect to turn 'rogue states' (whether they are functional or not) into failed states—which is what the US has done to Iraq—and to prevent failed states from developing into rogue states, which is the effective impact of US interventions in Afghanistan and Somalia. Imperialist military interventions employ a carrot-and-stick approach, destroying forces to the extent that they resist, while attempting to build up a subordinate local client structure. The carrot side of this doesn't build functioning states, however, since it merely fosters the kind of aid dependency analysed in our previous chapter. That is, it neutralises nations rather than builds them up.

There has been much hand-wringing in the West about the 'lack of planning' for the occupation that followed the invasion. There was indeed almost none, because the occupation was an accidental, if inevitable, consequence of the main plan, which was to destroy Saddam Hussein's Iraq, in order to reinforce US global strategic hegemony. President George W. Bush, admitting his naivety in foreign affairs, had run for office explicitly promising to give responsibility for foreign policy to his Vice President, Dick Cheney. Cheney was by all accounts obsessed with toppling Saddam, almost immediately nonsequitously proposing this as a response to September 11. Cheney's agenda was that already codified by the Project for the New American Century, to which Cheney was an original signatory, in the late 1990s, to ensure American dominance by removing hostile powers. This aim was in tune with the desire of the US public after 9-11 to control the world to the extent that future terrorism would be prevented. It was not in tune with opinion in much of the rest of the world, for the obvious reason that it was American exceptionalism that disregarded anyone else's interests, but from the point of view of American biopolitics, all life outside was relevant only to the extent that it served American life. The US during the Bush-Cheney era disregarded the objections of any erstwhile ally who sought to oppose its aggressions.

Once it had conquered Iraq, the Bush-Cheney regime set about destroying all forces there that opposed them. This contrasts with the behaviour of British occupation troops, who were concerned mainly to ensure civil peace in their zone: Britain's war aims were effectively more limited than America's, extending to removing Hussein, not to hunting down all possible traces of 'Terror' at a substate level. America sought to set up a pliant pro-American client state, but there were inadequate social forces to be rallied to such a purpose. While the Kurds were won over to a pro-American position during the long war on Iraq, the Arab majority of Iraqis have never been pro-American. America manages to dominate other Arab countries through the sponsorship of hereditary monarchies (in the Gulf) or the military (in Egypt). In Iraq, the monarchy had been long abolished (though the US reportedly considered reviving it, it had no base of support left),[54] and the military had been deliberately smashed by the US because it had been Hussein's own main power base. The absolute majority of Iraqis are Shia Arabs, who could be expected to welcome the removal of the Sunni dictator Hussein, but to become pro-American is a different thing. The only Shia-ruled state in the world, Iran, who Shia Iraqis naturally look to for guidance, is an implacable enemy of the US.[55]

After the best part of a decade of occupation, America decided to quit Iraq in the face of an insurgency that it to some extent brought to heel but could never vanquish. By the 2008 presidential election there was a bipartisan consensus for withdrawal. The cost in American lives of the occupation served no purpose other than continuing to destroy an already destroyed country, turning American public opinion against it.

America's adventure in Iraq had long since achieved its main goals. It aimed neither at stability for Iraq nor to improve Iraqi biopolitics, only to neutralise a threat. The current situation in Iraq is more desirable from a US point of view than the status quo ante bellum. The result of elections in Iraq has been Shia-dominated, pro-Iranian governments, which is in itself undesirable from the US point of view, but it is not clearly worse for them than Saddam Hussein's Arab nationalist government which opposed Israel and America's main Arab allies, despotic hereditary monarchies. It may be more desirable, because Shia Islam is less capable of uniting Iraq as a nation than was Arab nationalism, since a larger majority of Iraqis are Arab than are Shia. The country is now much more internally divided than before: the pro-American Kurds now effectively govern themselves, controlling enormous oil reserves. Regardless, the US has destroyed Iraq's capacity to be threatening, or indeed to operate without Western assistance.

Things have, at the time of writing in late 2014, in some respects changed dramatically in the last few months when the soi-disant 'Islamic State' (IS) has seized control of large parts of western Iraq, supported by a fresh local Sunni uprising. This has sufficiently alarmed American and other Western opinion to prompt a new intervention, mostly by air, however, without an official return of ground troops. What is important here is that this Western intervention came quite explicitly when the IS began to seize land from the Kurds—including threatening Kurdish oil production and facilities (the US was content for IS to seize oil facilities from the Syrian regime, but not from their Kurdish allies). The official casus belli for the West was the threat to religious minorities, specifically the Yazidi, by IS. One can contrast this to the lack of Western response to the persecutions of religious minorities, including Christians, by similar forces in Syria in the years running up to this, and the lack of Western concern about the growth of IS in Iraq until it began to make incursions into Kurdish areas. I will return to the topic of IS in the next section.

The inability of the Iraqi army to challenge the IS is a testament to the extraordinary current weakness of the Iraqi state. Hussein managed to keep the majority of the population in line with his military, whereas now even the majority cannot bring a minority to heel.

In light of such events, one might be tempted to agree with Gianni Vattimo that 'Iraq was a state in which people of different ethnic origins and religious traditions were put together only in order to create unstable conditions, thus necessitating the intervention of the West'. But this is inaccurate. While it is certainly true that the Western carve-up of the world in the colonial period has produced post-colonial states with borders largely indifferent to the creation of inter-ethnic tensions within and across states, inter-ethnic strife in Iraq did not necessitate, or even play a role in causing, Western intervention. Rather, the West fed tensions between social groups in Iraq in their attempt to weaken and remove Saddam Hussein's regime. The West invaded because, despite the interethnic rivalries, the Ba'ath Party was able, through biopolitics and increasingly through thanatopolitics, to impose enough national unity to remain a geostrategic threat to Western interests.

When the US withdrew from Iraq, it did so in favour of a stronger commitment to its ongoing occupation of Afghanistan: this was Barack Obama's explicit election platform in 2008. Afghanistan has often been cast as the 'good war' in contrast to

Iraq: a legal war against terrorists rather than against a sovereign state, directly related to 'September 11'. While the war in Afghanistan might be less flagrantly illegal and more closely connected to 9-11, it is in fact ultimately both illegal and not directly connected to that event. It is essentially the same as any other imperialist war, directed against Third World sovereignty and Third World biopolitics. The Taliban was the closest thing to a cohesive and autochthonous state that had formed in Afghanistan for two decades when the West invaded. Nato forces have since spent 13 years trying to destroy the Taliban, but it has continued throughout, for all its considerable shortcomings, to manifest itself as the main political force in the country. All that Nato has achieved is smashing Afghanistan.

As in Iraq, the initial justification for the invasion, in this case the search for the perpetrators of September 11, was quickly forgotten. The narrative changed to one of establishing human rights and democracy against the Taliban. The vacuousness of this narrative is apparent as soon as one scratches at it: any concern with the rights of Afghan people would augur strongly against imposing values and a government on them by force. Moreover, the Taliban are hardly more egregiously anti-women, anti-liberal or anti-democratic than the government of Saudi Arabia, a key Western ally. Western talk about human rights is just cant. Malala Yousafzai, a child who was engaged in Western sponsored education activism, was shot by the Taliban for her activities, and was held up in the West as an example of the Taliban's inhumanity. She was flown to Britain for care, even as Western drones slaughtered other children of her region. Biopolitics is for allies, thanatopolitics for everyone else. She was made part of a First World population, because simply existing in Pakistan exposed her to an undue risk of death.

Why then have Western forces remained? As in Iraq and Vietnam, they have stayed so long because at any given point withdrawal opens up the space for the establishment of an anti-

Western government that could serve as a base for operations against Western populations. The longer our troops stay, the more they destroy, the longer this moment of reckoning is put off. We pretend we are reconstructing Afghan society, but as in Iraq this is largely false.

5.2 Iraq and the Levant

After withdrawing from Iraq in 2011, America gave its blessing to efforts to destablise Iraq's neighbour Syria. For a time, this seemed to follow the same pattern of successful imperialist intervention against Libya in 2011: support internal opposition, then bomb regime forces. A casus belli in the form of alleged chemical weapons attacks blamed on the regime was produced in 2013, and Obama sought permission from Congress to begin bombing. Opposition in Congress and from foreign governments, particularly Russia, diverted Obama from this path and instead he reached a negotiated agreement that Syria would dispose of its chemical weapons. The bipartisan domestic US opposition represents a considerable war weariness in America. It also reflected some concern about the composition of the rebel forces in Syria, which have been committed entirely to an ideology of Sunni extremism almost since the beginning of the civil war, and which contain the very groups, principally Al-Qaeda, with whom America is supposed to have been at war since September 11.

One could suggest some in America have learnt the lesson of the 'blowback' from American sponsorship of Islamist militants against the Soviet Union in Afghanistan in the 1980s, among them Osama bin Laden, alleged architect of September 11. However, this connection is actually quite tenuous, bin Laden's role in the jihad against communism being marginal, and his relation to September 11 unproven (no was never tried in court; he publicly consistently denied responsibility, though recordings of private statements have surfaced in which he apparently claimed it).

I think no such lesson has been learnt: US policy continues to follow a logic that the enemy of our enemy is our friend, because this is entirely adequate for its purposes. The US previously sponsored Saddam Hussein when Iraq was fighting Iran in the 1980s. They did not thus create a decisive victory, but rather poured more oil on the fire, harming both sides. The US and Britain during this time blocked UN resolutions condemning Iraq for using chemical weapons, thus supporting his WMD programme when it suited them. It has been alleged that during the occupation of Iraq, the US actually at times armed and supported the militants who would go on to form the IS in the hope that they would turn their arms on other anti-US insurgents.[56] The West backed the Syrian opposition, even though it was Islamist and anti-Western in orientation, much as they had supported the Afghan mujahidin in the 1980s. Assad was initially at least the greater threat, because his Syria is an organised military state. That there was prevarication about whether it was actually desirable to aid the rebels against Assad in Syria in 2013 is thus due to the fact that it was becoming immediately unclear whether it was the Syrian government or the rebels that was the major threat to the US—and that this was so because the Syrian state's capacities had already been massively degraded in the civil conflict. Once the so-called Islamic State emerged out of this conflict as an organised force constituting itself in something like a state form, America began to back its main enemy, the Iraqi state. It has not yet fundamentally shifted its attitude towards the Syrian state, and voices from across the political spectrum in the West continue to call for the US to broaden its air strikes to attack Syrian government forces as well as the IS, thus in favour of smaller rebel groups opposed to IS. Since the US is already bombing multiple rebel groups in Syria, not only IS but also Al-Qaeda linked forces (in line with its longstanding global policy of trying to kill any member of Al-Qaeda located anywhere in the Middle East), this threatens to turn into a situation where the US is simply bombing anyone and everyone in Syria.[57] This indeed would not be as absurd as it sounds (though I do not believe it would happen—the US will of course always want to at least claim that there is a positive alternative it is supporting), since it follows the underlying logic of destruction which undergirds the US's militaristic foreign policy. Similarly, it is no problem for the US that while it bombs IS to protect Kurds in Syria and Iraq, its Nato ally Turkey is bombing Kurds across the border in its own territory.

On the occasion of the IS's seizure of Mosul, President Obama proclaimed that 'no one has an interest in seeing Iraq descend into chaos'. This statement is both carefully phrased and disingenuous. Obama's primary meaning is that America is opposed to the appearance of an anti-American extremist state in Iraq, which is true, but indeed not a matter of chaos, but of an anti-American order. The very fact, moreover, that he feels the need to clarify that America does not seek to foment chaos in Iraq indicates that America might be thought to have an interest in doing so, not least because it fomented chaos in Syria, which catalysed instability in Iraq in turn, and more generally because American policies have produced the contemporary regional situation. Obama is protesting too much: even though everyone involved, America, the Iraqi state, and IS, would rather achieve their goals without chaos, in practice the triangular contestation of these different forces is what produces it. Hence America effectively does have an interest in seeing chaos in Iraq, because the solidification of a pro-Iranian government is contrary to US objectives, just as the formation of the so-called Islamic State is. So America tries to have it both ways, tries to remove the current government as a condition of bombing IS forces, turning chaos into an order to its liking.

All this makes perfect sense from the point of view of the goal of furthering US geopolitical hegemony. If it does cause terrorism against the US as blowback, this terrorism justifies further imperialist war. This, at the level of the strategy of power, is all mutually complementary. This does not imply that the US deliberately creates terrorism to justify its imperialism, only that its imperialist policies are generated within a situation that they perpetuate, and which perpetuates them in turn. Again, however, if it is not deliberate, it is at least a case of indifference. If it was vitally important to the US that Iraq not be destabilised, America might have been more cautious in encouraging rebellion in Syria. But it was indifferent to the consequences for Iraq, just as it was indifferent to the devastating impact of war on the lives of Syrians. Surely, however, we can say that America is concerned to prevent terrorism against its population? Indeed it is, but this basic biopolitical concern extends to a protection of the 'homeland', and not to the negation of the extension of American imperial power outside it, precisely because this power follows a logic of interests that serves the population: withdrawal from the world would not be to the obvious overall benefit of the US population from a biopolitical point of view, even if it would negate that actually relatively tiny risk to American lives posed by terrorism. And of course there are also enormous economic and political interests not reducible to biopolitics in play.

I do not ascribe inerrancy to America and its allies, nor to imperialism itself. Surely they can and have made mistakes, and ultimately are doomed to fail catastrophically at some point. There is no guarantee, indeed, that terrorism will always incite imperialism, though its tendency to do so makes it a self-contradictory form of anti-imperialism. There are examples in which one could argue that terrorism has been 'successful' in achieving its aims. One is the Madrid bombings of 2004, which caused a change of government and thus Spanish withdrawal from Iraq. This must be understood, however, in a context in which the Spanish populace had not previously been attacked from this quarter and hence, unlike the US population, never sanctioned their country's role in attacking Iraq. The Spanish thus viewed the bombings not as part of a war, but as the result of unwarranted Spanish aggression, hence saw withdrawal as the best form of protection.

5.3 Death Trade

We have in the last two sections given examples of the active destabilisation of Third World biopolitics through the use of First World arms, both in Western hands and as military aid passed into the hands of others. The supply of arms from the First World to the Third is not always so selective—indeed, it performs its destabilising task precisely by not being selective. Of course, the West does not sell its weapons to just anyone, but rather to other states primarily—still, it does this indiscriminately enough that weapons are used in conflicts that kill large numbers of people around the world. This trade makes a mockery of the already risible attempts at aiding the Third World.

Most First World countries, with the important exception of the US, recognise domestically the extent to which weapons are inimical to biopolitics. Yet, all the big Western economies and several others—America, Britain, Germany, France, Israel, and even that pillar of social democracy Sweden—have sizable arms manufacturing businesses that are major export industries. Indeed, with aircraft and automobile manufacture, and the production of machine tools, modern weaponry is one of the few areas of manufacturing industry still substantially based in the First World. Imperialist wars are in effect live tests and sales displays for deadly commodities.

5.4 Environmental Devastation

I will end this chapter by dealing with what is actually perhaps the most pressing form of degradation of Third World biopolitics, the destruction of the environment. I include it under the heading of 'war' because it is like war metaphorically speaking a flow of death outward from the First World to the Third.

Climate change is clearly the most dangerous single form of environmental damage. It will affect the Third World disproportionately, yet has been and is being caused disproportionately by the First World: until 2012, each First World country was producing more CO_2 per capita than any Third World country, generally by an enormous margin. As of 2012, China has reached a per capita CO_2 production level higher than those of the Mediterranean European countries, though there is a question, which we will consider below, of whether in light of such developments China remains a Third World nation. It should be noted, however, that these measures of per capita production are misleading, inasmuch as China emits much of its greenhouse gases to produce goods that are then consumed by First World people.

Regarding the disproportionate effects, the Third World is mostly tropical, the zone of the world where temperature rises are least welcome. But it is poverty rather than mere geographical location that primarily makes the impact of climate change likely to be so much more devastating for the global poor. We in the First World have the well-built houses and elasticity in food supply, hence can weather this not-so-metaphorical storm. We will be inconvenienced, but the poorest will be likely simply to die.

Ever since the scientific consensus about the reality of anthropogenic climate change emerged, the attitude of the First World towards it has been the indifference towards the lives of the global poor characteristic of biopolitical imperialism.   First World behaviour in relation to climate change is often defined as 'inaction', but it is objectively an active programme of creating climate change. To characterise it as inaction implies that the First World continuing to do the same things year after year, including increasing its economic product, is nothing, when in fact it is relentlessly destructive activity.

In the two decades since 1990, large emissions falls have

occurred only in Second World countries, and there only because the restoration of capitalism caused economic collapse. At the other end of the spectrum, Australia, the world's greatest per capita environmental vandal, increased its emissions by more than 50 per cent in this period. Other Western countries with very large rises include Canada (over 20 per cent), Greece (almost 30 per cent), Ireland (more than 30 per cent), New Zealand (almost 35 per cent), Norway (more than 30 per cent), Portugal (more than 35 per cent), and Spain (closer to 40 per cent). Western countries with substantial falls are the exception: they are namely Germany (more than 20 per cent), Sweden (more than 20 per cent), and the UK (more than 15 per cent). The German case is explained largely by the fact that Germany is an agglomeration of two 1990 states, one of which was Second World. The UK case is explained by the aggressive deindustrialisation its government pursued in the 1980s, which of course does not mean it does not consume industrial goods and in that sense cause emissions, only that it does not directly emit them from its own national territory. Sweden is thus unique as a country that reduced domestic emissions without significant deindustrialisation. Still, its 20 per cent reduction, even if replicated across the Western world, would inadequate to address the problem of climate change. Thus, Sweden is still climatically imperialist, since it has continued actually to wreck the climate.

One might argue that politicians and publics in the First World have behaved as they have because they genuinely do not believe that climate change is happening. Such politicians are thankfully few in this century in most First World countries, though in the US and Australia climate change deniers still occupy positions of real influence. I would suggest, however, that there is an important difference between people not believing in climate change before evidence is widely available, and their actively disbelieving it in the face of widely established evidence. Some climate change deniers disbelieve generically in almost all facts asserted by orthodox science and the mainstream media. But denialist politicians and publics are not generally of this ilk. Their disbelief is peculiar denial of the facts of climate change, which is self-serving and shows characteristic callousness towards the well-being of people in the Third World.

Western countries act selfishly both chronologically and geographically: their emissions harm people in the future and people in other places. However, the harm that they visit on the future is different to that they do to the Third World. That is, the *sine qua non* of Western public policy is maintaining GDP growth. Thus, future Westerners will be richer (on average) than current ones. So, while the environmental conditions of the future will be worse than today, we will also have more wealth to mitigate the consequences for ourselves. This only holds true assuming the continuation of imperialism, which will allow the West to continue to monopolise the resources of the whole world even as the climate collapses, enforcing our monetary advantage to take resources from the Third World even as mortality there increases.

This does not mean that the First World will never act on climate change: it is indeed in its interest to prevent it, but only if it does not have to sacrifice its wealth accumulation to do so. Moreover, efforts to act on climate change will themselves proceed through the circuits of imperialism, in the form of carbon offsetting and carbon trading, for example. We are already seeing land being bought in poorer regions of the world to grow forests to offset carbon dioxide emissions in the West. In the proposed monetised global marketplace of emissions, it seems likely that the pressures for changed land use and resource assignment will indeed kill poor people, much as the shift to biofuels already has done.

6

Resistance

How can one both make a biopower function and exercise the rights of war, the rights of murder and the function of death, without becoming racist? That was the problem, and that, I think, is still the problem. – Michel Foucault

Foucault ends *Society Must Be Defended* with this suggestion. I think we may read it in two ways. Very literally, one may, as I have tended to in earlier writings of mine, take it to define the problem with which we must wrestle: given the existence of this binary politics of life and death, how can we avoid racism? I think it can also be read in a different, more ironic way, however, as suggesting that the problem is that people struggle to make biopolitics and thanatopolitics work together without racism when in fact this is a forlorn enterprise, and that we are missing the bigger problem, which is not racism itself but the existence of this binary which requires it.

As foreshadowed at the outset, I will provide no solutions to the problems I have outlined in this book. I do not believe it is possible to make reliable predictions about or prescriptions for the future because of the complexity of society. We can make projections based on what will happen if current trends continue, but we know from experience that trends typically do not continue. I will conclude only by surveying two things. One is the way in which the situation of biopolitical imperialism may be said to be changing and to have changed today already in the era of neoliberalism. The other is the possible and historic resistance to biopolitical imperialism.

6.1 Neoliberalism

Neoliberalism has been haunting this book, mentioned regularly throughout, but never explored. Neoliberalism is in short the contemporary faith in market mechanisms and the private sector as the best way to run any industry or service. Strictly speaking, this is true only of an extreme version of neoliberalism that has come to prominence in recent decades. Earlier forms of neoliberalism denigrated the state less, holding up the market model as artificial, whereas contemporary neoliberals are closer to classical liberals in thinking markets to be natural and states artificial. This not-so-neo-liberalism has replaced the mid-twentieth century doxa that relatively strong state guidance was required to run economies effectively.

Contemporary neoliberalism does not necessarily presage the end of biopolitics as such, but it does threaten the existence of the universal welfare state. It has already produced an increasingly striated biopolitics. The poorest receive dwindling benefits. Most people in Western countries still continue to rely on national social insurance schemes for retirement, invalidity, illness, and unemployment, but recent developments threaten to break this apart. Increasing numbers of people have private pensions, health and employment insurance, meaning they no longer rely on public biopolitics, weakening their solidarity with the poorest who do. States increasingly outsource social welfare functions to charities, threatening the replacement of state protection with discretionary charitable assistance: witness the massive rise of the use of charitable 'food banks' by the British poor in recent years. The extent to which any biopolitics can completely cut out the poor is limited to some extent by the risks local poverty poses, from criminality and disease most obviously. The only way that the state could treat its underclass as it treats the Third World would be if technologies were developed that could shield the rich from the poor within the nation just as effectively as distance and borders shield us from the Third World, although the elites in the Third World seem to get away with quite astonishing levels of rapacity and indifference towards their populations.

In this relation we may refer to the 2011 urban rebellions in England. The killing of one young man by police was enough to spark these. They were a response to police harassment, to austerity, and many other things—but they were also riots in defence of the biopolitical-thanatopolitical boundary, to say that we cannot, will not be killed summarily by the state. While judicial vengeance was swift, I doubt that the lesson was entirely lost on the powers that be, that the Metropolitan Police will be so quick to kill poor British people for a while. And yet, as CCTV and gates and security guards bloom around buildings and communities, at some point thanatopolitics may make a comeback on the streets of London.

Neoliberalism is linked to the diminution of the nation state, which is to say to globalisation. Its clarion call for labour deregulation is made explicitly on the basis of 'international competitiveness'. Now, this seems like a nationalistic calculation: our nation must compete. But in reality the nation is subordinated here to the needs of transnational finance capital. National divisions allow capital to pit people against one another in a race to the bottom. The anti-globalisation struggle that briefly flowered at the turn of the millennium incorporated manifold tendencies, including both the defence of national autonomy in relation to capital and the call for an 'altermondialisation' which would assert a higher authority over capital. These remain the two possible directions of resistance to globalisation, and are not necessarily mutually exclusive. We are today in a situation of twin decline of nation state and biopolitics, though there remain substantial forces defending each of these.

Resistance to dismantling biopolitical structures is inevitable. It seems that battles already fought in the twentieth century for biopolitical protections are now being fought in reverse as rearguard actions against austerity by the left. The austerity programme conducted in most Western countries in recent years constitutes in effect nothing less than the managed transfer of wealth from the poor to the rich. It is a bailout of the wealthy, of the finance industry, of shareholders, at the expense of ordinary people. Of course, nationalist discourse is mobilised here: David Cameron told us that we are 'all in it together'.

His logic is not entirely disingenuous. The level of financialisation of the UK economy is such that it is not in the interests of the nation to allow banks to go bust. The transfer from poor to rich to keep the banks going is necessary because the banks are the engine of the economy. They do not literally produce what keeps the country going, but via the repatriation of profits through investments and earnings from financial services they do provide the lifeblood of the British economy. Of course, it is possible to reorganise society and the economy so this it would no longer be based on this sector.

In other Western countries, the financial sector does not have the same weight, but nonetheless the same broad principle applies: the economic system is dependent on profitability, so this must be maintained at any cost. While austerity is everywhere justified on the basis of the economic impact of the 2008 financial crisis, one should note, however, the case of Australia, which has had austerity during this period, even though its economy has remained robust. The major political parties here declare that there is a crisis in budgetary receipts, but this has been created not by economic conditions so much as through tax cuts, that is, by transferring wealth to the rich.

In addition to the managed transfer of wealth to them by the state, the wealthy have in recent decades increasingly simply bypassed the state through exotic tax arrangements. As Ronen Palan notes, this change did not proceed smoothly, and indeed was facilitated primarily by the British state during its period of economic financialisation, against the efforts of the US state to keep control of its citizens' tax receipts.[58] Imperialism itself thus increasingly bypasses biopolitics and the state.

We might expect growing inequality and attacks on welfare, as well as the bypassing of the state, to put tension on the solidarity of the imperialist proletariat with its rulers. Still, this does not seem yet to have happened decisively anywhere, and there is no telling when or whether it will.

6.2 Beyond Imperialism

How to combat imperialism? As Chomsky is fond of saying, if the West wants to stop terrorism, its first step should be to stop supporting it. We can say the same thing about Third World poverty. In both cases, we can go further, to a single demand: stop intervening. This does not mean refusing disaster relief, nor not participating in the eradication of communicable diseases, nor refusing to share knowledge. It means stopping invading Third World countries, stopping bombing them, stopping giving them 'aid', stopping intervening in their politics.

Now, I do not mean this as a serious policy suggestion so much as, like Chomsky's, a polemical remark. There is little reason to imagine that the West will adopt such policies; at least, not on the basis of the picture I have painted in this book, which claims that our interventions in the Third World are effectively in our own interest.

The most politically influential arguments for non-intervention mounted within First World polities come from the extreme right, which claims precisely that non-intervention is in the interests of First World notions. Both libertarians and neofascists argue that aid to and military adventures in the Third World are a waste of First World money and lives. I reject the framework of premises from which these arguments are mounted. Nonetheless, were libertarians, for example, to implement their vision in America, even if it would be a catastrophe for the American economy and American biopolitics, it might be a relief for the victims of US imperialism. However, there is scant chance of this happening, and at present the rhetoric of the far right is not a contender for genuine implementation, rather serving as a marginal voice which contributes to the overall direction of politics in the compromise direction of attacks on biopolitics at home, coupled with imperialism abroad, though one may credit right-wing libertarianism with a role in marshalling opposition to America's recent wars.

An argument for non-intervention in accordance with the perspective of this book would have to be either altruistic, based on self-sacrifice within the existing system, or premised on a different way of living than the instrumentalism of contemporary capitalist Western societies. Either would seem to require a reorganisation of society, since our system does not seem capable of genuine altruism insofar as it is fixated on economic growth and profits.

Imperialism is not unambiguously beneficial for the people of imperialist states, but rather only seems so on the basis of a specific conception of the good proper to biopolitical capitalist society, which equates it to monetary wealth and longevity. In the choice between belonging to the First or Third World within the imperialist situation, the choice is clear. But this is not the alternative we are entertaining, which is between life within imperialism and life beyond it. The First World worker after imperialism may be materially poorer, but this may not matter if society is reorganised so that there are less tangible gains, from living in a fundamentally different way to the nihilistic materialism that increasingly characterises all existing societies.

Explicitly left-wing anti-imperialist movements within the metropoles seem by and large to understand precisely this. Critical analyses of imperialism like the present one come from this milieu. This in itself demonstrates that people do not always follow their own material interests, narrowly construed. Still, the calculus of narrow, material interests has become hegemonic and doubtless such interests exert a powerful motivational pressure in any culture—hence perhaps the relative scarcity of objections, theoretical or activist, to imperialism within metropolitan societies. While anti-war movements have at times been non-trivially influential, they have always in First World countries tended to be minority movements which wield an influence as a consideration for policy makers via their capacity to cause disorder rather than directly changing government decisions through democratic institutions. They have only been genuinely mass movements capable of stopping wars by toppling governments in situations, such as Germany in 1918, of mass conscription where the imperialist power is losing a war.

This does not prove that mass anti-imperialist movements within the metropoles are impossible, but neither do we have reason to expect them to occur. There is some possibility of change both in the deluded right-wing movements mentioned earlier, and in radical movements, for example, the environmentalist movement, that would reduce the size of First World economies and militaries. But in the end change seems more likely to come from the resistance of the Third World, both because there self-interest is on the side of anti-imperialism, and because empirically, mass anti-imperialist movements have repeatedly emerged there.

Third World anti-imperialism has historically taken the form of nationalism, which of course implies certain generic dangers, most obviously the stifling of alterity within the territory of the posited nation, and it has also had great disasters. The worst cases are Khmer Rouge-controlled Cambodia (Kampuchea) and North Korea.

Kampuchea is generally understood as a deliberate genocide by evil men. I would argue the reality is closer to a tragedy brought about by a collision of extremely weak (rather than strong) central authority, a fantasy of absolute self-sufficiency, and the sudden removal of US aid from a population absolutely dependent on it.[59] That is, the Khmer Rouge proposed to run a country entirely autonomously in a situation where this was completely impossible, because the country was war ravaged and all necessary technical skills, including knowledge of how to govern a country, were lacking, with the population being dependent for its survival on aid from outside. In the absence of any functioning biopolitics or the requisite know-how to establish one, and simply of enough food, Khmer Rouge rule was essentially thanatopolitical. This meant enormous numbers of deaths, as people were forced to work and exterminated for failing to become the image they were supposed to embody.

Large numbers of people have died in North Korea too in recent decades. The North Korean regime has also made a fetish of self-sufficiency, under the title of 'Juche', elevating this principle to replace Marxism as the official national ideology. Despite this, the country long remained dependent on support from the Soviet Union. When the USSR collapsed, North Korea was forced to fall back on its own resources. If there was a single reason that this led to famine, it was that the regime subordinated food production to maintaining its military. Unlike the Khmer Rouge, who did not seem to grasp the rudiments of biopolitics, the North Korean regime followed a biopolitical logic in sacrificing much of its population in the name of defending it. However, North Korea is not governed in the interests of its population. Alongside its paranoid hermeticism, it exhibits another common—even ubiquitous—tendency of anti-imperialist nationalism, namely corruption. North Korea's *nomenklatura* are so corrupt their rule is scarcely distinguishable from feudalism. Indeed, it is unclear that North Korea now remains biopolitical at all, and its national logic seems to have long since become defence of the Kim dynasty, not the population.

These are the worst cases of anti-imperialism. An example where biopolitics has been consistently prioritised is Cuba. A rather different example of Third World nationalist anti-imperialism that did not collapse in on itself is provided by China.

Rather, it collapsed outward, in the opening of the Chinese economy. I have suggested above that China's historic anti-imperialism produced a robust state that could resist the depredations of imperialism to a large degree once the economy was opened. While it might seem that China's rise is now assured, the future remains opaque and the prognosis for Chinese development unclear. The Chinese boom has mostly been driven by manufacturing exports to the West, which the West has not yet paid for. There is no ultimate enforcement mechanism for the First World's debts to China, hence the former could renege, albeit at the risk of being cut off from a supplier of cheap goods upon which it might now be said to be dependent. Perhaps China retains enough of the character of a command economy that it can deal with a decline in Western demand for its produce by redirecting production towards domestic consumption, but this is untested.

We are below the historic peak of anti-imperialist struggle. This is partly because anti-imperialism has been discredited by the implosions and explosions of anti-imperialist states, and for the prosaic reason that many historic anti-imperialist movements were anti-colonial, and the abandonment of the tactic of colonialism has successfully defused resistance to imperialism. Still, anti-imperialist struggle continues. It has risen to previously unseen prominence in Latin America in the last decade, in a context where colonialism has been absent from most countries for two centuries and where the US's post-colonial imperialism is widely understood as such. One may also point to the continuing growth of political Islam, which has been more or less explicitly anti-imperialist in complexion, during the same period.

It is hard to know how to assess the prospects for change in Latin America. There is some sign of supranationalism in anti-imperialism here, although the main expression of this, Mercosur, is a free-trade bloc. Venezuela, at the radical extreme of recent attempts at social change and anti-imperialism in Latin

America, has made significant gains in biological parameters, though not noticeably greater than other countries in the region with less radical programmes, and Venezuela has latterly faced severe economic difficulties. We may say, however, that regional biopolitical gains are spearheaded by Venezuela in the sense that concessions are being made everywhere because of the threat represented by Chavez's Bolivarian Revolution, and that the economic difficulties of Venezuela are caused by the reaction to this, the attempt by capital to make Venezuela's economy scream and stifle this regional beacon of socialism. Thus, the prognosis for revolutionary change in Latin America is unclear, but I would suggest that in the struggle between pro- and anti-imperialist— which are also in this case pro- and anti-capitalist—forces, the battlelines have at least been drawn.

At a certain point in the last decade, Maoist insurgencies in South Asia also seemed to be making crucial progress. In Nepal, Maoists seemed poised for military victory in the civil war, and then parlayed their position into a compromise with less radical communist parties to produce a new republican constitution. This, however, has led to an as-yet interminable period of wrangling and contestation of power within a constitution drafting period that has lasted for more than six years. Nepal's importance, and indeed the freedom of action of its government, is moreover limited by the fact that it is completely surrounded by two giant neighbours, China and India—China's border with Nepal being high Himalaya, India essentially has the power to force Nepal to do whatever it wants. The main game is thus Maoist rebellion in India itself, which has been continuously in existence for four decades, and in the last decade went through a significant period of consolidation and expansion of territory, but nonetheless remains confined to (vast) forest areas. Its prospects are intriguing not least because the absence of communist revolution might be a salient difference between China's capacity to develop and India's, though the conditions in contemporary

South Asia are entirely different to those that obtained in China when it had its Maoist revolution.

Such internecine movements that never seriously threaten to take state power have significant similarities with terrorism, and indeed rebels are always cast as terrorists. Terrorism—as the term is today usually understood, viz. to mean substate actors using terror as a weapon against a population—is ineffective as a means of pursuing political change. This is not to say that movements that begin as terrorist cannot become something else, but terroristic methods are desperate acts of violence perpetrated in an attempt to compensate for lack of support. Suicide bombing is perhaps the apogee of terrorism in both its capacity to terrorise and its self-undermining pointlessness. This technique apparently turns the indifference of imperialism towards Third World lives back against it. Rather than allowing these lives to be simply ignored, it turns them into a weapon. In doing so, it is profoundly anti-biopolitical: it says, you value your lives so much, but we do not care about ours, we will lay down our lives to kill you. This willingness to die is peculiarly terrifying to biopolitical sensibilities. This however plays directly into the dehumanisation of its enemies by biopolitical society. Suicide bombing demonstrates to the population the absolute savagery of the bomber, and reinforces the idea that the enemy's life has no value since that enemy herself does not value it. This logic is that expressed by General William Westmoreland, the US commander in Vietnam during the peak period of US involvement, even before suicide bombing was invented: 'The Oriental doesn't put the same high price on life as does a Westerner... We value life and human dignity. They don't care about life and human dignity'. Westmoreland used this orientalism to justify the savage slaughter of people by the US military in Vietnam, on the basis effectively that they themselves did not care whether they lived or died.

For citizens of the First World, whose lives are valued by the state, quite different avenues of biopolitical resistance are open. Perhaps the classic use of life as a weapon of resistance in this context is in hunger strikes. These challenge authorities to concede to prisoner demands in order to meet their duty to keep prisoners alive. Recently, this has been employed by prisoners, many of whom are from the Third World, at Guantanamo Bay. While these prisoners are the type of people America executes extrajudicially elsewhere in the world, as captives on American soil they cannot be killed so easily. The captors' solution is force-feeding—an elegant solution exploiting the fact that, while the authorities cannot allow these prisoners to die, it seems that they can subject them to inhuman treatment that would not be allowed with US citizens. Such resistance is only possible within a biopolitical situation. Iraqis could not resist Western sanctions by going on hunger strike, since the problem was precisely that the imperialists were indifferent to their hunger.

An extraordinary form of anti-imperialist action at the intersection of the two worlds is the deliberate offering by First Worlders of their inviolate, biopolitically protected lives as a protection to the lives of people in the Third World. The best known case of this is perhaps the 'human shield' action in Iraq in 2003 against the US invasion. This was effective insofar as US forces went out of their way to avoid harming the 80 Western human shields in the country. The human shields were located often in crucial pieces of biopolitical infrastructure, such as food distribution, water treatment, power production, and communication facilities, and thus may have saved these from destruction. They used their biopolitical privilege to preserve the biopolitics of Iraq. The genius of this human shield initiative is that the shields were largely from the same countries involved in the attack. One may compare this unfavourably to the fate of Westerners dealing with the Israeli military, which has a number of times deliberately and at close quarters killed First World foreigners standing with Palestinians.

6.3 Globalise Biopolitics

The obvious demand to raise against biopolitical imperialism, certainly from the point of view of abolishing its racism, is to remove the distinction between the population and its outside. The abolition of borders to the movement of people is considered a fringe demand today, despite the fact that there were no such borders until a little over a century ago.

In reality, anti-border campaigns, though they aim at a borderless, stateless world, operate as pressure groups for slightly looser borders. The main constituency challenging the border is made up of the immigrants and would-be immigrants who try to circumvent it, who are similarly dealt with either by harsher restrictions, or slight loosenings. It is hard to see any amount of pressure decisively bringing down the borders around biopolitics, since it is manifest that allowing people in the Third World untrammelled access to First World biopolitics would put intolerable pressure on the latter, since it is a privilege premised on the exclusion of the mass of humanity, a privilege most people in the First World wish to maintain.

We are moving in the direction of the opening of borders to physical movement without opening the biopolitical borders. Through the increasing striation of access to welfare, people can be allowed to move freely without placing pressure on biopolitics. Thus, in America, the most biopolitically striated nation, immigration amnesty can occur, because residency doesn't guarantee much state aid. The gates go up around houses and communities, hospitals and schools, rather than countries.

One could argue that such liberalisation of the movement of people would expose the existing system's iniquity: rather than dying out of sight in foreign lands, the global poor would die outside the gated communities of the rich. One might also suggest that a global labour market might catalyse the formation of genuinely international labour and political movements. However, I do not believe either consequence will follow automatically: as long as biopolitics remains striated, we are caught in neoliberal individualisation that inhibits solidarity from forming. With Étienne Balibar, we can suspect that racism in our society will be overcome through absolute individualisation, with each person treated so differently that there is no racial pattern. But this does not solve anything, so much as obscure things. We cannot simply place our faith in the Marxian logic that capitalism will produce its own gravediggers.

The obvious alternative to apartheid is a genuinely universal, global biopolitics. However, there is simply very little hint of this emerging in the existing situation, although there are those who advocate global government, and it may one day come to pass. The extension of government across rich nations, say in Europe, is not a significant step in the direction of globalising biopolitics—if anything this tends in the opposite direction, by consolidating First World privilege. Moreover, even the European Union is not yet a truly biopolitical framework.

There is today a minor worldwide biopolitical apparatus that coordinates international attempts to combat particular diseases. The most concrete component of this is the World Health Organisation (WHO). This may be seen as a global proto-biopolitics, inasmuch as similar specific measures were found at the genesis of national biopolitics. As in those national cases, the motivation at this pre-biopolitical stage is only to help the poor in order to protect the privileged. First World governments' investment in curing malaria might seem altruistic since it does not affect their populations directly. However, even if malaria is not currently in the Global North, it might spread there with climate change, and malaria also catalyses the spread and emergence of other diseases that do threaten the North such as AIDS.

In Australia in 2014, on the occasion of the first ever mass outbreak of the Ebola virus in West Africa, idiosyncratically there has been a left-right split in Australian attitudes, between a right-wing government that has refused to send medical personnel to help on the basis that it will not put its citizens in harm's way, and a left-wing opposition that demands, in line with the policies of most governments internationally, including the US and the Conservative government in the UK, that Australia should send help. The argument to send help, however, is not cast in altruistic terms, that the scale of human suffering requires it. Indeed, this would not make sense, since many other diseases in Africa, such as malaria, kill many more people than Ebola (although this may change depending on the unfolding of the epidemic), and are not treated as an emergency by the West. Rather, it is argued that the disease must be combatted in West Africa to *prevent its spread* to Western nations. Effectively, both sides argue about the best way to protect our citizens, with any concern for the citizens of African nations being barely discernible.

Disease, hunger, etc. in the Third World moreover threaten to create disorder with economic, political, and demographic impacts on the First World. This provides a possible vector for the expansion of biopolitics worldwide, through the establishment of global governmental institutions in a dialectic of struggle with the global population, but this has yet to begin decisively as a process. It is hard to see where the impetus for such an establishment would come from in the current situation. There are demands from people in the Third World for better conditions, but there is no global agency to address this demand to. The widespread failure of Third World governments to address biopolitics is endemic and has meant that 'civil society' demands are often addressed to First World governments, First World NGOs, and international organisations dominated and funded by the First World. Demands made to such institutions, however, are almost unavoidably invitations for more imperialism. The nation remains the more likely structure through which biopolitics in the Third World might progress, as it has been recently in Latin America, with a global dimension built only by demands transmitted thereby later.

6.4 Beyond Biopolitics?

Since this is a book about biopolitics, it has focused on metrics of life. This is not meant to imply that politics can be reduced to such measures, or to biopolitics. Biopolitics can only care for life; it does not give meaning to life. Biopolitics becomes nihilism when it becomes the *sine qua non* of politics, when life is imagined as the goal itself.

However, there is no significant politics today that does not incorporate biology. Only the extreme fringe of right-wing libertarianism tends in the direction of not assigning a biopolitical role to the state, though we could say it imagines, like left libertarianism, that biopolitics can exist without the state. Religious ideologies that seem to be indifferent to death seem to be 'anti-biopolitical', though I am dubious whether they really are. Some tiny death cults may constitute exceptions, but it seems to me that major religious political movements, including, for example, extremist Salafist/Takfirist Sunni Muslims, actually champion the welfare of a putative population. The most substantial genuinely anti-biopolitical strand today is the very marginal anarcho-primitivist movement, which opposes civilisation and technology as such. Giorgio Agamben's critique of a millennia-long 'biopolitics' seems to me to share no small affinity with this strain.

We can expect that there will someday be something beyond biopolitics, but it is not at all clear what it would look like. Anti-biopolitical tendencies, be they libertarian, primitivist, or conservative, advocate not going beyond biopolitics so much as returning to a (mythicised) past before biopolitics. The goal of reactivating older forms of life might seem to have in its favour the fact that these forms of life have previously been shown to work. However, reactivating these in the current situation, with all its social and technological differences, is prima facie unlikely.[60] More plausible is the attempt to move beyond to something new. Yet, it does not seem to me that anyone is trying such a thing, or that it is even possible today to think what it might look like. The abolition of biopolitics (in the Foucauldian sense) seems to have as its only available meaning the reactionary project of restoring pre-biopolitical society.

So what can we demand? More and different biopolitics. The demand for biopolitics need not imply absolute biopolitics, the abolition of death. Rather, biopolitical demands are typically for specific uses of biopolitics. Any anti-imperialism today must take the form of demands for new biopolitics, though it is of course not my place to say what people in the Third World will or should demand.

There is nonetheless a specific biopolitics I am concerned to criticise: Western social democracy, because of its interpenetration with imperialism. The extent to which social democracy is necessarily imperialist is an open question, but it is historically a compromise built around imperialism. Social democratic nostalgia is a ghost haunting the left today. It is a feeling in the grassroots, among ordinary people, voters, unionists, party members, even while most of the paid politicians of the 'centre left' are today neoliberals, and the political activists of the far left are revolutionary socialists supposedly without illusions about social democracy. The ghost takes concrete form in campaigns that are merely 'against cuts' or 'against austerity'. Understandable though these may be, they cannot but imply a call for the restoration of a status quo ante neoliberalism. I do not condemn anti-austerity campaigns, but wish to point out their conservatism in relation to imperialism. Calls in the First World for the restoration of social democracy are not anti-imperialist, but in effect a demand for the restoration of a component of imperialism. Concrete avatars of this nostalgia in the public sphere are, for example, Owen Jones in Britain, or, in Germany, Axel Honneth. Jones seems to me a peculiarly prominent figure locally arguing for little more than the good old days, even if he says many important things eloquently. Honneth does something rather similar, though his perspective is much more sophisticated. Social democracy for Honneth is no end in itself, but a pathway to the evolution of a society of greater recognition than we have ever experienced. While this is not the place to refute his claims for the progressive potentials of social democracy, I think the narrative I have put tends to contradict such a view social democracy.

Notes

1. For fairly comprehensive surveys of this history, see Thomas Lemke, *Biopolitics: An Advanced Introduction*, New York: New York University Press, 2011, and the first chapter of Roberto Esposito, *Bìos*, Minneapolis: University of Minnesota Press, 2008, pp. 13–23.

2. An excellent survey of the emergence of this concept and subsequent debates can be found in Anthony Brewer, *Marxist Theories of Imperialism*. London: Routledge, 1990.

3. Michael Hardt and Antonio Negri, 'Why We Need a Multilateral Magna Carta', *Global Agenda*, 2004.

4. 'A 25-year gap between the life expectancy of rich and poor Londoners is a further indictment of our unequal society', *The Independent*, 15 January 2014, http://www.independent .co.uk/voices/comment/a-25-year-gap-between-the-life-expectancy-of-rich-and-poor-londoners-is-a-further-indictment-of-our-unequal-society-9061888.html

5. Esposito, *Bìos*, p. 16. Esposito's determination of biopolitics as having to do with immunity is itself, however, apparently organicist, meaning to this extent that he is not part of the critique of biopolitics either.

6. Zak Cope, *Divided World Divided Class*, Montreal: Kersplebedep, p. 8.

7. Michel Foucault, *Society Must Be Defended*, New York: Picador, 2003, p. 257.

8. See Francisco Bethencourt, *Racisms: From the Crusades to the Twentieth Century*, Princeton: Princeton University Press, 2014.

9. Michel Foucault, *The Order of Things*, London: Tavistock, 1970, p. 84; Bethencourt 2014, p. 247 ff.

10. 'The Affordable Care Act and African Americans', US Department of Health and Human Services Fact Sheet, 2014

http://www.hhs.gov/healthcare/facts/factsheets/2012/04/aca-and-african-americans04122012a.html

11. I am grateful to Douglas Moggach for pointing this out to me.

12. Lake and Reynolds, *Drawing the Global Colour Line*, Cambridge: Cambridge University Press, 2008, p. 26.

13. Ibid., p. 282.

14. Ibid., p. 30.

15. For a discussion of this, see David R. Roediger, *The Wages of Whiteness*, London: Verso, 2007, pp. 8–9.

16. Lake and Reynolds, op. cit., p. 156.

17. Ibid., p. 158.

18. Ibid., p. 32.

19. Ibid., p. 220.

20. John Solomos, *Race and Racism in Britain*, Basingstoke: Palgrave Macmillan, 2003, p. 45.

21. Ibid., p.42.

22. Evan Smith and Marinella Marmo, *Race, Gender and the Body in British Immigration Control*, Basingstoke: Palgrave Macmillan, 2014, p. 6.

23. Solomos, op. cit., p. 54 ff.; see also Evan Smith and Marinella Marmo, 'The myth of sovereignty: British immigration control in policy and practice in the nineteen-seventies', *Historical Research*, 87:236, 244–269, 2014, p. 5.

24. Lake and Reynolds, op. cit., p. 159.

25. William Walters, 'Mapping Schengenland: denaturalizing the border', *Environment and International Biopolitics Planning D: Society and Space*, 20, 2002, 561–580.

26. James North, 'How US Foreign Policy Created an Immigrant Refugee Crisis on Its Own Southern Border', *The Nation*, 9 July 2014, access date 12 July 2014 http://m.thenation.com/article/180578-how-us-foreign-policy-created-immigrant-refugee-crisis-its-own-southern-border

27. Donald G. McNeil Jr, 'Cuba's Fortresses Against a Viral Foe',

New York Times 7th May 2012, access date 9 October 2014 http://www.nytimes.com/2012/05/08/health/cubas-aids-sanitariums-fortresses-against-a-viral-foe.html?

28. M Goyal, RL Mehta, LJ Schneiderman, AR Sehgal, 'Economic and Health Consequences of Seeking a Kidney in India', *JAMA*, 2002, 288(13), 1589-93.

29. Donna Dickenson, *Body Shopping: The Economy Fuelled by Flesh and Blood*, London: Oneworld, 2008, p. 9.

30. Ibid., p. 5.

31. Ibid., p. 6.

32. Ben Doherty, 'Drug companies "using Indians as guinea pigs"', *Sydney Morning Herald*, 27 January 2013, http://www.smh.com.au/world/drug-companies-using-indians-as-guinea-pigs-20130126-2dduh.html

33. David B Resnik, 'The Ethics of HIV Research in Developing nations', *Bioethics*, 12:4, 1998.

34. Melinda Cooper, *Life as Surplus*, Seattle: University of Washington Press, 2008, p. 52.

35. Eileen O'Grady and Stephan Lefebvre, 'There Has Never Been a Better Time to be Forced into Exile for Being Gay in Honduras', *Center for Economic and Policy Research*, 20 June 2014

36. Dan Collyns, 'Quinoa brings riches to the Andes', *The Guardian*, 15 January 2013, accessed 9 October 2014, http://www.guardian.co.uk/world/2013/jan/14/quinoa-andes-bolivia-peru-crop

37. Shayana Kadidal, 'Subject-Matter Imperialism? Biodiversity, Foreign Prior Art and the Neem Patent Controversy', *IDEA – The Journal of Culture and Technology*, 37:2, p. 378

38. Mike Davis, *Late Victorian Holocausts*, London: Verso, 2001, p. 299.

39. Emily S Cassidy, Paul C West, James S Gerber and Jonathan A Foley, 'Redefining agricultural yields: from tonnes to people nourished per hectare' *Environmental Research Letters*,

8:3, 2013

40. Lisa Griffin, 'The New Fishing Imperialism', UCL Development Planning Unit, 13 September 2012, accessed 12 July 2014, http://blogs.ucl.ac.uk/dpublog/2012/09/13/the-new-fishing-imperialism/

41. Craig Burnside and David Dollar, 'Aid, Policies, and Growth', *The American Economic Review* 90:4, 2000, pp. 847-868

42. Muhammad Umair Mushtaq, 'Public Health in British India: A Brief Account of the History of Medical Services and Disease Prevention in Colonial India', *Indian J Community Med.* 2009; 34(1): 6–14.

43. 'The long march to universal coverage: lessons from China', The World Bank, 1 January 2013, http://documents.world bank.org/curated/en/2013/01/17207313/long-march-universal -coverage-lessons-china

44. Howard W. French, 'Into Africa: China's Wild Rush', *New York Times*, 16 May 2014 http://www.nytimes.com/2014/ 05/17/opinion/into-africa-chinas-wild-rush.html

45. 'Hurun Report Chinese Luxury Consumer Survey 2014', 16 January 2014, http://www.hurun.net/en/ArticleShow.aspx? nid=262; 'The Great Chinese Exodus', *Wall Street Journal*, 15 August, 2014, http://online.wsj.com/articles/the-great-chine se-exodus-1408120906?

46. In this estimate I include suicides and homicides by firearm, though it should be noted that the former outnumber the latter 2:1.

47. Michael Dillon and Julian Reid, *The Liberal Way of War*, London: Routledge, 2009, p. 43.

48. 'Radio warns Afghans over food parcels' BBC News, 28 October 2001, http://news.bbc.co.uk/2/hi/world/monitoring/ media_reports/1624787.stm

49. 'Cashless in Gaza?', secret communiqué from US State Department office, Tel Aviv, Israel, 3 November 2008,

https://wikileaks.org/plusd/cables/08TELAVIV2447_a.html#
efmAB5ACKAgIAja

50. Eric Rouleau, 'The View From France: America's Unyielding Policy toward Iraq', *Foreign Affairs*, 74:1, January/February 1995.

51. Carl Conetta, 'The Wages of War', *Project on Defense Alternatives*, 20 October 2003, http://www.comw.org/pda /0310rm8ap2.html#1.%20Iraqi%20civilian%20fatalities%20in %20the%201991%20Gulf

52. Noam Chomsky, *Deterring Democracy*, New York: Vintage, 1992, p. 410.

53. Barry S Levy and Victor W Sidel, 'Adverse health consequences of the Iraq War', *The Lancet*, 381:9870, 2013, pp. 949–958. There has been much debate about the scale of mortality caused by the invasion. This gives a relatively conservative estimate. Others have estimated closer to half a million deaths: A Hagopian, A Flaxman, TK Takaro, SAE Al Shatari, J Rajaratnam, S Becker, *et al.* 'Mortality in Iraq Associated with the 2003–2011 War and Occupation: Findings from a National Cluster Sample Survey', *PLoS Med* 10(10), 2012.

54. Aslam Khan, 'US plans to merge Iraq, Jordan after war', *Centre for Research on Globalisation*, 26 September 2002, http://www.globalresearch.ca/articles/KHA209A.html

55. One could argue Syria is also in a sense 'Shia-ruled', if one defines Alawites as Shi'ite, and define them as a ruling group; it too is in any case anti-American enough for the Americans to agitate for the removal of its regime.

56. Nafeez Ahmed, 'How the west created the Islamic state', *Counterpunch*, 12–14 September 2014, http://www.counter-punch.org/2014/09/12/how-the-west-created-the-islamic-state/https://medium.com/@NafeezAhmed/how-the-west-created-the-islamic-state-dbfa6f83bc1f

57. Kathy Gilsnian, 'The U.S. Has Bombed Two Different Sides

in Syria's Civil War'. 23 September 2014, http://www.theatlantic.com/international/archive/2014/09/the-us-has-bombed-multiple-sides-in-syrias-civil-war/380660/

58. Ronen Palan, 'The New Dependency Theory', *Irish Left Review*, 15 January 2013, http://www.irishleftreview.org/2013/01/15/dependency-theory/

59. See Philip Short, *Pol Pot*, New York: Henry Holt, 2006. Short further claims that Cambodian Buddhist culture also played a factor in the brutal thanatopolitics of the Khmer Rouge, though I am wary that this smacks of neo-racist orientalism.

60. Primitivists argue that environmental collapse will guarantee that we have to go back—but this is not clear either. That is, it is not clear at all that we will simply be thrown backwards technologically by collapse, but rather humanity may continue to survive and develop technologically even in the face of a serious environmental crisis that kills billions of us.

Contemporary culture has eliminated both the concept of the public and the figure of the intellectual. Former public spaces – both physical and cultural – are now either derelict or colonized by advertising. A cretinous anti-intellectualism presides, cheerled by expensively educated hacks in the pay of multinational corporations who reassure their bored readers that there is no need to rouse themselves from their interpassive stupor. The informal censorship internalized and propagated by the cultural workers of late capitalism generates a banal conformity that the propaganda chiefs of Stalinism could only ever have dreamt of imposing. Zer0 Books knows that another kind of discourse – intellectual without being academic, popular without being populist – is not only possible: it is already flourishing, in the regions beyond the striplit malls of so-called mass media and the neurotically bureaucratic halls of the academy. Zer0 is committed to the idea of publishing as a making public of the intellectual. It is convinced that in the unthinking, blandly consensual culture in which we live, critical and engaged theoretical reflection is more important than ever before.

ZERO BOOKS

*If this book has helped you to clarify an idea, solve a problem or extend
your knowledge, you may like to read more titles from Zero Books.
Recent bestsellers are:*

Capitalist Realism Is there no alternative?
Mark Fisher
An analysis of the ways in which capitalism has presented itself as
the only realistic political-economic system.
Paperback: November 27, 2009 978-1-84694-317-1 $14.95 £7.99.
eBook: July 1, 2012 978-1-78099-734-6 $9.99 £6.99.

The Wandering Who? A study of Jewish identity politics
Gilad Atzmon
An explosive unique crucial book tackling the issues of Jewish
Identity Politics and ideology and their global influence.
Paperback: September 30, 2011 978-1-84694-875-6 $14.95 £8.99.
eBook: September 30, 2011 978-1-84694-876-3 $9.99 £6.99.

Clampdown Pop-cultural wars on class and gender
Rhian E. Jones
Class and gender in Britpop and after, and why 'chav' is a
feminist issue.
Paperback: March 29, 2013 978-1-78099-708-7 $14.95 £9.99.
eBook: March 29, 2013 978-1-78099-707-0 $7.99 £4.99.

The Quadruple Object
Graham Harman
Uses a pack of playing cards to present Harman's metaphysical
system of fourfold objects, including human access, Heidegger's
indirect causation, panpsychism and ontography.
Paperback: July 29, 2011 978-1-84694-700-1 $16.95 £9.99.

Weird Realism Lovecraft and Philosophy
Graham Harman
As Hölderlin was to Martin Heidegger and Mallarmé to Jacques
Derrida, so is H.P. Lovecraft to the Speculative Realist philoso-
phers.
Paperback: September 28, 2012 978-1-78099-252-5 $24.95 £14.99.
eBook: September 28, 2012 978-1-78099-907-4 $9.99 £6.99.

Sweetening the Pill or How We Got Hooked on Hormonal Birth
Control
Holly Grigg-Spall
Is it really true? Has contraception liberated or oppressed
women?
Paperback: September 27, 2013 978-1-78099-607-3 $22.95 £12.99.
eBook: September 27, 2013 978-1-78099-608-0 $9.99 £6.99.

Why Are We The Good Guys? Reclaiming Your Mind From The
Delusions Of Propaganda
David Cromwell
A provocative challenge to the standard ideology that Western
power is a benevolent force in the world.
Paperback: September 28, 2012 978-1-78099-365-2 $26.95 £15.99.
eBook: September 28, 2012 978-1-78099-366-9 $9.99 £6.99.

The Truth about Art Reclaiming quality
Patrick Doorly
The book traces the multiple meanings of art to their various
sources, and equips the reader to choose between them.
Paperback: August 30, 2013 978-1-78099-841-1 $32.95 £19.99.

Bells and Whistles More Speculative Realism
Graham Harman
In this diverse collection of sixteen essays, lectures, and inter-
views Graham Harman lucidly explains the principles of

Speculative Realism, including his own object-oriented philosophy.
Paperback: November 29, 2013 978-1-78279-038-9 $26.95 £15.99.
eBook: November 29, 2013 978-1-78279-037-2 $9.99 £6.99.

Towards Speculative Realism: Essays and Lectures Essays and Lectures
Graham Harman
These writings chart Harman's rise from Chicago sportswriter to co founder of one of Europe's most promising philosophical movements: Speculative Realism.
Paperback: November 26, 2010 978-1-84694-394-2 $16.95 £9.99.
eBook: January 1, 1970 978-1-84694-603-5 $9.99 £6.99.

Meat Market Female flesh under capitalism
Laurie Penny
A feminist dissection of women's bodies as the fleshy fulcrum of capitalist cannibalism, whereby women are both consumers and consumed.
Paperback: April 29, 2011 978-1-84694-521-2 $12.95 £6.99.
eBook: May 21, 2012 978-1-84694-782-7 $9.99 £6.99.

Translating Anarchy The Anarchism of Occupy Wall Street
Mark Bray
An insider's account of the anarchists who ignited Occupy Wall Street.
Paperback: September 27, 2013 978-1-78279-126-3 $26.95 £15.99.
eBook: September 27, 2013 978-1-78279-125-6 $6.99 £4.99.

One Dimensional Woman
Nina Power
Exposes the dark heart of contemporary cultural life by examining pornography, consumer capitalism and the ideology of women's work.

Paperback: November 27, 2009 978-1-84694-241-9 $14.95 £7.99.
eBook: July 1, 2012 978-1-78099-737-7 $9.99 £6.99.

Dead Man Working
Carl Cederstrom, Peter Fleming
An analysis of the dead man working and the way in which
capital is now colonizing life itself.
Paperback: May 25, 2012 978-1-78099-156-6 $14.95 £9.99.
eBook: June 27, 2012 978-1-78099-157-3 $9.99 £6.99.

Unpatriotic History of the Second World War
James Heartfield
The Second World War was not the Good War of legend. James
Heartfield explains that both Allies and Axis powers fought for
the same goals - territory, markets and natural resources.
Paperback: September 28, 2012 978-1-78099-378-2 $42.95 £23.99.
eBook: September 28, 2012 978-1-78099-379-9 $9.99 £6.99.

Find more titles at www.zero-books.net